For 2006 Returns

CLERGY TAX

J. David Epstein
Tax Attorney

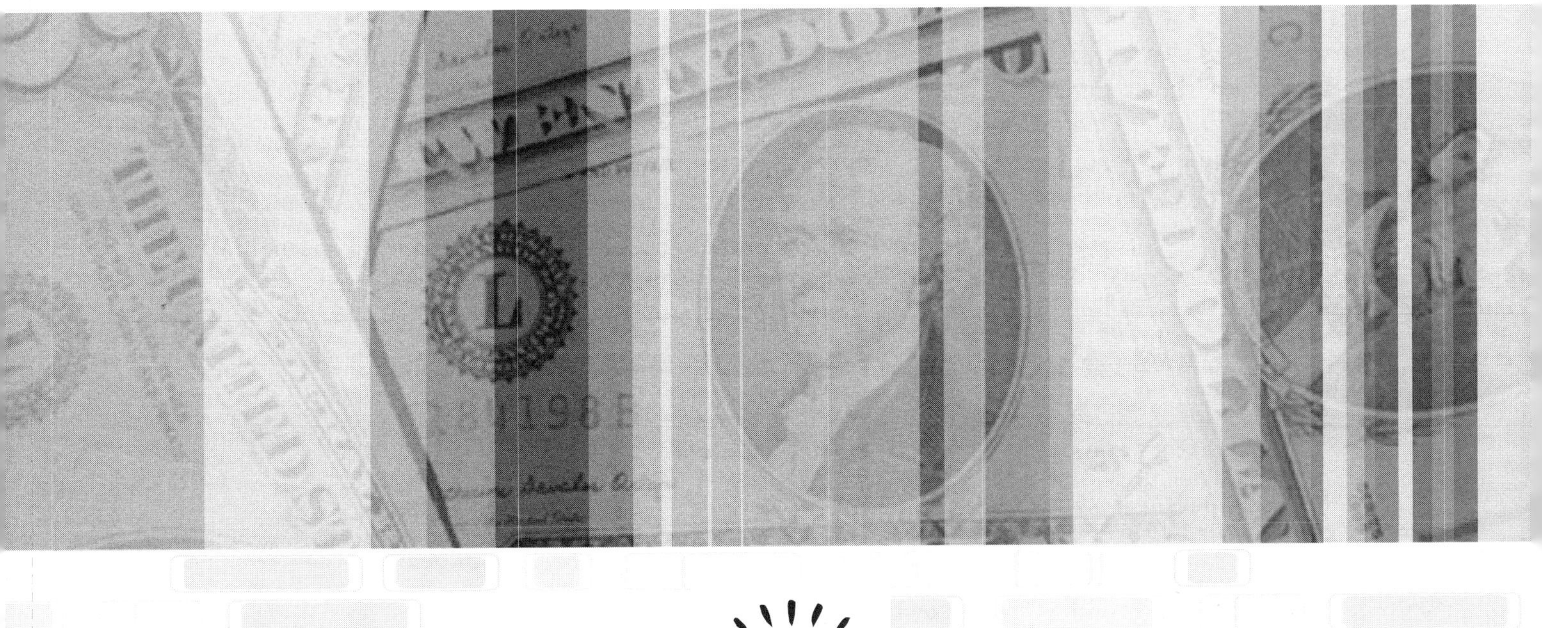

Gospel Light

PUBLISHED BY GOSPEL LIGHT
VENTURA, CALIFORNIA, U.S.A.
PRINTED IN THE U.S.A.

Gospel Light is a Christian publisher dedicated to serving the local church. We believe God's vision for Gospel Light is to provide church leaders with biblical, user-friendly materials that will help them evangelize, disciple and minister to children, youth and families.

It is our prayer that this Gospel Light resource will help you discover biblical truth for your own life and help you minister to others. May God richly bless you.

For a free catalog of resources from Gospel Light, please call your Christian supplier or contact us at 1-800-4-GOSPEL *or* www.gospellight.com.

PUBLISHING STAFF

Dr. Elmer L. Towns, Senior Consulting Publisher • **Bayard Taylor, M.Div.,** Senior Editor, Biblical and Theological Issues

ISBN 0-8307-4300-6
© 2006 J. David Epstein, J.D.
All rights reserved.
Printed in the U.S.A.

LIMITED WARRANTY—PLEASE READ BEFORE USING THIS PRODUCT

Because tax laws are inherently complex and may not be completely free of doubtful interpretations, you are advised to verify your work and determine that the tax rules you are following do in fact apply to your situation.

In no event will Gospel Light be liable for direct, indirect, special, incidental or consequential damages arising out of the use, inability to use or inappropriate use of the documentation herein, even if Gospel Light is advised of or aware of the possibility of such damages. In no case will Gospel Light's liability exceed the amount of the purchase price paid for this product.

Gospel Light in no way guarantees or warrants any particular tax or other result from the use of the *Clergy Tax* program.

Although *Clergy Tax* attempts to provide accurate and authoritative information regarding the subject matter covered, it is sold with the understanding that Gospel Light is not engaged in rendering legal, accounting or other professional services; and it is sold subject to the foregoing limited warranty. If legal, accounting or other expert assistance is required, the services of a competent professional person should be sought.

Note: The forms in this resource are provided as samples only and are not to be used as final forms. Contact the IRS at 1-800-829-3676 or visit the IRS website at www.irs.gov for final forms.

No returns will be accepted on this item after April 15, 2007.

COPYRIGHT NOTICE

Permission to make photocopies or to reproduce by any other mechanical or electronic means in whole or in part any designated* page in this book is granted only to the original purchaser and is intended for noncommercial use. None of the material in this book may be reproduced for any commercial promotion, advertising or sale of a product or service, or to share with any other persons, churches or organizations. Sharing of the material in this book with other churches or organizations not owned or controlled by the original purchaser is also prohibited. All rights reserved.

*Only pages with the following notation can be legally reproduced:

© 2006 J. David Epstein, J.D. Permission to photocopy granted. *Clergy Tax 2007*

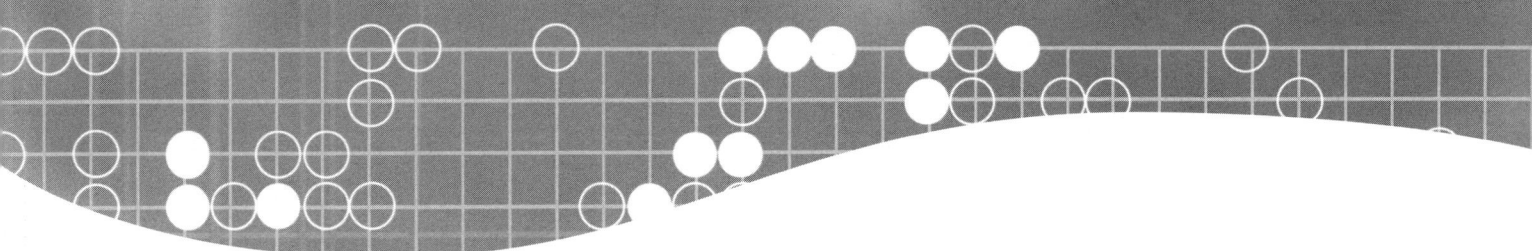

CONTENTS

Letter to the Pastor 5

Part 1 7
The 12 Boxes You Need to Fill Out Your Tax Return

Part 2 29
Items That May Not Apply to All Pastors

Appendix 1 43
Checklists of Deductions for Ministers

Appendix 2 51
State Filing Requirements

Appendix 3 53
Sample Tax Forms

Appendix 4 61
How to Handle 1099s

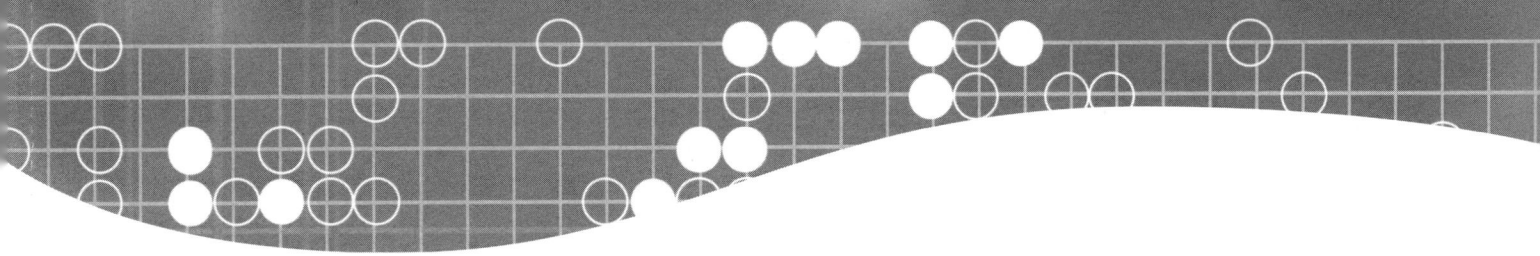

LETTER TO THE PASTOR

The *Clergy Tax* system has helped tens of thousands of pastors just like you to conquer tax time each year. Most pastors don't have time to learn all the complicated IRS rules for clergy (although many of these rules contain golden nuggets of tax savings!), and with *Clergy Tax*, you don't have to. To prepare an IRS-correct return, you only have to find the numbers for 12 *Clergy Tax* Boxes.

The idea behind *Clergy Tax* is "paint by numbers." You only need about 12 numbers to fill out your tax return. *Clergy Tax* takes you step-by-step, shows you what each of the 12 numbers is and tells you exactly how to determine it. The worksheets make the process easy, and most of the 12 numbers are already at your fingertips in the tax documents you get at the end of the year. But it's fair to tell you that a few of them are harder to find, and one in particular is going to be hard for those ministers who don't keep very good records: the amount you spent for housing allowance.

The better your records are organized, the easier it's going to be to prepare your tax return each year. If you have good records, *Clergy Tax* will help make it all so very easy. Even if you don't have good records, *Clergy Tax* will point the way for you and help you collect the information you need and then show you exactly where to put it. Basically all you have to do is find the 12 numbers, plug them in to your tax return and then you're done!

In the past year, there have been quite a few changes to the Tax Code that affect ministers, and I highlight these for you throughout the book. Here are several ways that *Clergy Tax* helps you:

- It helps you have a stealth tax return—the directions help you avoid red flags, which lowers your audit profile; this helps you have a tax return that's nearly invisible to the IRS.
- It helps point you toward the lowest tax position for a minister in your particular financial situation. (Ministers using the *Clergy Tax* system for the first time have often reported saving hundreds of dollars on their taxes.)
- It is updated each year to reflect the latest tax law changes.

As an added protection for ministers, I have run the rules in *Clergy Tax* by the tax authorities in the IRS National Office, as well as key IRS-exempt organizations experts in other parts of the country. They did not find anything that they disagreed with (actually, they did find one or two things initially, all in favor of the minister, but we made the changes they recommended). I've also run the rules you read here by a number of other tough critics, to see if there might be any areas we could improve on.

How This Book Is Organized

Part 1: The 12 Boxes You Need to Fill Out Your Tax Return

This section shows you the 12 boxes most ministers need to complete their tax returns. Worksheets guide you to filling out many of the boxes. Look for the ✎ icon—this Form Key will indicate a number that needs to be entered on a tax form (or perhaps on a worksheet in the book).

After you complete Part 1, you will probably be 90- to 100-percent finished with your tax return, unless you have a lot of complicated issues.

Part 2: Items That May Not Apply to All Pastors

The items in Part 2 won't apply to every minister; however, it's a good idea to scan the list to make sure none of the scenarios applies to you. If you find anything in the list that does apply, simply follow the directions for that item.

The Appendices

- Appendix 1 gives you a handy quick-reference checklist of deductions for ministers (so you don't overlook anything).
- Appendix 2 offers some helpful state-filing information (however, if you use tax-preparation software, the software probably has this information built in).
- Appendix 3 gives you sample tax forms to refer to, along with instructions on how to get less common forms if you need them.
- Appendix 4 walks you through the special rules for ministers who receive Form 1099.

Using *Clergy Tax* with Tax-Preparation Software

You can use *Clergy Tax* even if you are planning on using a computerized tax program (which can do the math for you) or filing your taxes online. You'll have the numbers you'll need at your fingertips. Just plug them in and voilà! you're done.

What You'll Need to Prepare Your Return

Are you ready for the list of what you'll need before we get started? Don't let its brevity fool you; each element in this short list is important.

- Your last year's federal and state tax returns (If you didn't file your taxes last year, consult a competent tax professional immediately.)
- Your church's payroll sheet (if one was kept for you)
- All of this year's Form W-2s, 1099s and 1098s (for your mortgage interest and taxes) that you've received

Valuable Tips

- The information you use to prepare your tax return must be true and complete *to the best of your knowledge*. If information needed to complete your return is missing or destroyed, simply do your best to make the most accurate good-faith estimate that you can.
- Save *all* notes and papers you use to prepare your tax return each year, including your good-faith estimate notes. Keep these papers as long as you keep the return itself.
- Make a photocopy of your return. It is better to have an exact copy rather than the common practice of just keeping a penciled-in version.
- If you have a tax refund due this year, the IRS will send it to you *unless* you designate that the refund be applied toward your taxes for next year. (To do this, enter part or all of your refund on your Form 1040, Line 75.) You can also ask that your refund be direct deposited to your bank account: just fill in lines 74b, 74c and 74d, or use form 8888.
- Start a file at the *beginning* of each year for all tax-related papers! When you receive anything that you even suspect you will need for your taxes, put it in this file. You'll have everything ready when tax time rolls around again.

When It's All Said and Done

Use the tools and knowledge you will gain from this edition of *Clergy Tax* to begin your tax planning for next year. You have the rest of the year for the *Clergy Tax* system to help you analyze your tax situation and point out ways to lower your tax and keep a lower audit profile. In your church, for example, you may want to do a complete salary restructuring to increase your benefits and lower your taxes, or completely revamp the accounting system so that your minister's tax information is better organized at the end of the year.

PART ONE

THE 12 BOXES YOU NEED TO FILL OUT YOUR TAX RETURN

Start with a Correct Form W-2

First, to have a correct tax return, you must have a correct W-2. If your W-2 is wrong, your tax return will be wrong, too—and that could lead to big surprises if you're audited.

A Note About 1099s: If you still want to have a 1099 after reading the first part of the 1099 appendix of this book (appendix 4), follow the directions in the last part of that same appendix.

To have a correct W-2, use the simple Box 1 worksheet starting on page 8. Fill in the numbers, add them up, and you should have the right W-2 for a minister. It's a good idea to go through the worksheet, and then compare the results to the W-2 you actually got from your church. If the two numbers do not match, you should use the number from the worksheet; you may also want to have your church file a corrected W-2 for you by using IRS Form W-2c.

Note: You can use the numbers from the W-2 Worksheet on your tax return, even if your church did not issue you a W-2.

Look for the pencil icon (✎) throughout the book. This Form Key indicates information regarding on which form and on what line a particular number goes. It's paint-by-number easy. **Important:** Some of the 12 Boxes go in more than one place or on more than one form. Be sure to read the directions carefully so that you don't miss anything.

Note: Appendix 3 contains a sample Form W-2 and a sample tax return (Form 1040, Schedule A, Schedule B and Schedule SE). These forms will cover the needs of most ministers.

If a Form Key goes to a form that is not shown in appendix 3, this means that the form isn't used very much by ministers. To get any of these kinds of forms, go to http://www.irs.gov/formspubs/index.html and select the "Form and Instruction number" link.

Box 1: W-2 Income Worksheet

The number for Box 1 is the amount that should be on Line 1 of your W-2. (If you don't have a W-2, refer to the sample form on page 54.)

Here is what always goes in Box 1 (i.e., these items should have been included on Line 1 of your W-2). Add up the amounts as indicated on the following worksheet; then follow the directions for where to put the number:

Note: If you did not receive a W-2 from your church, refer to part 2, item 1 on page 31 for instructions. You'll still need the number from the Box 1 worksheet.

If you received a 1099, refer to appendix 4 on page 61 for instructions. You'll still need to use the Box 1 worksheet.

W-2 Income Worksheet

$_____ **Regular Salary that You Receive from Your Church** (*not* including your housing allowance)

$_____ **Christmas Bonuses**[a]

$_____ **Year-End and Birthday Bonuses**[a]

$_____ (If you own your car) **Auto Allowance Paid in Cash or by Check** (for which no mileage was turned in; if you got paid 44.5 cents per mile by the church for miles you drove on church business, then you don't have to put this amount in Box 1)

$_____ (If the church owns your car) **Personal Use of the Church Auto** (use the Annual Lease Value Worksheet—see page 26)

$_____ **Life Insurance Premiums Paid by the Church** (*except* premiums for group term insurance up to $50,000 face amount and/or any policies from which the church gets the money after your lifetime)

$_____ **Travel and Clothing Allowance**[b]

$_____ **Personal Vacations Paid for by the Church**[c]

$_____ **School Tuition Paid by the Church for Your Children**[d] (if the children attended a school *not* related to your church)

$_____ **Social Security Tax Paid by the Church for You as a Minister** (on top of your regular salary)[e]

$_____ **Federal or State Income Tax Paid by the Church for You as a Minister** (on top of your regular salary)[e]

$_____ **Advances Received Against Your Salary** (even if they were called loans)

$_____ **Expenses Reimbursed Under a Nonaccountable Plan**[f]

$_____ **Excess Housing Allowance**[g]

=$_____ **Total**

✎ **This is Box 1.** (See "OK, I've got the number for Box 1. Now what?" on page 9.)

Notes for W-2 Income Worksheet

a. These are taxable even if they were collected as "love offerings."
b. These are all taxable items, even if they are listed as part of your housing allowance.
c. Personal vacations are time off during which you did not perform ministry.
d. See pages 43-44 for more information regarding church-paid school tuitions that may not be taxable.
e. This is not the same as Social Security, federal or state tax withheld from a minister's salary—it is tax paid on your behalf as a minister so that you don't have to pay it.
f. If your church does not have an accountable reimbursement plan, any amounts the church reimburses you for church-related or business expenses are taxable and must be reported. (You may still be able to deduct these expenses—see page 20. You can avoid this problem altogether by having a church Board meeting and adopting an accountable reimbursement plan.)
g. Add up how much you spent on housing items (use the Worksheet showing a list of housing items you can use). Subtract what you spent on housing items from the amount the church paid you for housing allowance. If the church paid you more for housing than you actually spent on housing items, the excess goes in Box 1. See Housing Item 4 on page 19.

"OK, I'VE GOT THE NUMBER FOR BOX 1. NOW WHAT?"

First, compare the number in Box 1 to the number on Line 1 of your W-2. Do they match? If so, great! If not, don't use your W-2 to fill out your tax return. Instead, use the number you just calculated for Box 1.

- Now, take the number for Box 1 and enter it on Form 1040, Line 7.
- Don't forget to carry the number from Form W-2, Line 2 to Form 1040, Line 64. (State income tax from Form W-2, Lines 17 and 19 goes on your state income tax return, if any, and also on Schedule A, Line 5 of your federal return.)

A Note About Earned Income Credit: If Box 1 plus your housing allowance is less than about $38,000 (depending on the number of children you have), you may qualify for the Earned Income Credit, a type of extra refund from the IRS. See the IRS instructions for more information.

What happens if you have a number on one of the lines in the worksheet, but it was left off your W-2? Can you spell S-I-B-E-R-I-A? Seriously, all you have to do is pick from one of the following options:

- **Option 1**—On your tax return, use the correct number you figured up for Box 1; then have your church file form W-2c to correct your W-2.
- **Option 2**—Use the W-2 your church gave you (even though it is incorrect); then enter the items that were left off your W-2 on Form 1040, Line 21. (If you are not Social Security tax exempt, you'll have to carry the amount from Line 21 to Schedule SE, Line 2.) You can attach the reproducible "Supporting Schedule to Form 1040, Line 21" worksheet on page 10 to indicate how you arrived at this number. Simply enter the amount from the worksheet on Line 21 and add the notation, "See attached schedule." Then make a photocopy of the worksheet, fill in the information as indicated and attach it to your tax return.

Supporting Schedule to Form 1040, Line 21

(Clergy Tax Box 1)

Name of Minister: _____

Social Security Number: _____ - _____ - _____

Note: The following items were not included on the W-2 issued by the church:

Excess Housing Allowance	$ _____
Christmas, Year-End and/or Birthday Bonuses	$ _____
Personal Use of Church Automobile	$ _____
Love Offerings	$ _____
Pay Advances	$ _____
Cash Automobile Allowance	$ _____
Clothing Allowance	$ _____
Life Insurance Premiums Paid by Church	$ _____
Social Security Tax Paid by Church	$ _____
Federal or State Income Tax Paid by Church	$ _____
Personal Vacations Paid by Church	$ _____
School Tuition Paid by Church for Pastor's Children's Attendance at Nonchurch School	$ _____
Expenses Reimbursed Under Nonaccountable Plan	$ _____
Other: _____	$ _____
= **Subtotal**	$ _____

Note: The following items were included erroneously on the W-2 issued by the _____ church and should be subtracted from the total:

Other: _____ $ _____

Other: _____ $ _____

= **Total** $ _____

Copyright © 2006 J. David Epstein, J.D. Permission to photocopy granted. *Clergy Tax 2007*

Box 2: Spouse's Church Salary and/or Spouse's or Minister's Income Earned Outside the Church

Spouse's Income from Church Salary

If your spouse earned a church salary in 2006, write that amount here (do not include any housing amounts):

$_____

- Add the number from his or her W-2, Line 1 to Form 1040, Line 7.
- Add the number from his or her W-2, Line 2 to Form 1040, Line 64.
- Add the number(s), if any, from his or her W-2, Lines 17 and 19 to Schedule A, Line 5.

Spouse's and Minister's Outside Income

Spouse's Income Earned Outside the Church

If your spouse earned a salary or other type of income from somewhere besides the church in 2006:

W-2 Income
- Add the number from his or her W-2, Line 1 to Form 1040, Line 7.
- Add the number from his or her W-2, Line 2 to Form 1040, Line 64.
- Add the number(s), if any, from his or her W-2, Lines 17 and 19 to Schedule A, Line 5.

1099 Income
- Add the 1099 amount to Form 1040, Line 21 and use the "Other" line of the Supporting Schedule to Form 1040, Line 21 for the total of your spouse's 1099 income. (**Alternative:** You can enter this income on Schedule C, Line 1 instead, but doing so will increase your chances of an audit.)

Minister's Income Earned Outside the Church

If you worked anywhere else besides the church in 2006:

W-2 Income
- Add the number from your W-2, Line 1 to Form 1040, Line 7.
- Add the number from your W-2, Line 2 to Form 1040, Line 64.
- Add the number(s), if any, from W-2, Lines 17 and 19 to Schedule A, Line 5.

1099 Income
- Add the 1099 amount to Form 1040, Line 21 and use the "Other" line of the Supporting Schedule to Form 1040, Line 21 for the total of your 1099 income from outside the church. (**Alternative:** You can enter this income on Schedule C, Line 1 instead, but doing so will increase your chances of an audit.)

Note: If you or your spouse received a 1099 *from your church* for work you did during 2006, refer to appendix 4, "How to Handle 1099s" on page 61. If the church is your main source of income, 1099s should be entered on Schedule C, Line 1. Appendix 4 will tell you how to do this.

Some tax practitioners think it is correct to report 1099 income on Form 1040, Line 21; others will tell you it has to go on Schedule C (which is more prone to being audited). In some cases, the location where income is reported can cause a "matching inquiry." This is merely a letter from the IRS because they can't figure out where you reported a certain amount of income, and these letters can be answered by mail.

Here is my position on where to report income on your tax return: As long as the income is reported correctly as to the amount, and as long as the correct tax is paid (income tax as well as Social Security tax, if it is due), it has been my experience that the IRS really doesn't care if you dotted every *i* and crossed every *t*. On Schedule C particularly, the IRS will often take the position with ministers that you can't use it anyway, even if the income you got was reported on a 1099. The big advantage to a Schedule C is that when you take expenses on that form, they count as deductions against both income as well as Social Security (or self-employment) taxes. The IRS doesn't like this and will often try to move that income somewhere else on your return so they can move the expenses to Schedule A where the government gets an advantage.

Note: You can still deduct your church-related business expenses from Schedule SE income even if you use Line 21 (see the instructions in Box 6 on page 14 for how to do this).

The bottom line is that if you report 1099 income on Form 1040, Line 21, the IRS isn't likely to care, and you get the added benefit of filing a return with a lower audit profile.

Box 3: Honorariums and Fees Paid Directly to the Pastor

Use this Box if you get a W-2 from your church, but also had either of these kinds of outside income.

Note: If these items went directly to the church, instead of to you, they are not income and don't have to be reported.

Box 3 Worksheet

$_____   **Honorariums Received for Outside Speaking**

$_____   **Fees Received for Weddings, Funerals, Baptisms and Masses**

✎ **This is Box 3.** Enter either of these items on Form 1040, Line 21. Write in the description of the income, and then fill in the amount.
If you are not Social Security tax exempt, also enter this income on Schedule SE, Line 2. (Don't carry this income to Schedule SE if you have filed Form 4361 to be exempt from Social Security tax.)

Box 4: Interest Earned

For this Box, you'll need each of the Forms 1099 you received from banks or companies that paid you interest in 2006.

Box 4 Worksheet

$ _____ Bank or Company: _____

$ _____ Bank or Company: _____

$ _____ Bank or Company: _____

= $ _____ Total

✏️ **This is Box 4.** Enter the total on Schedule B, Line 1 of your tax return (unless the interest is clearly marked as "non-taxable" on your form 1099). If this total is less than $1,500, you can just enter the amount on Form 1040, Line 8a.
   If the total is *more than* $1,500, also be sure to check the appropriate box(es) under Schedule B, Part III, Items 7 and 8.

Box 5: Dividends Received

For this Box, you'll need each of the Forms 1099 you received from banks or companies that paid you dividends in 2006.

Box 5 Worksheet

$ _____ Bank or Company: _____

$ _____ Bank or Company: _____

$ _____ Bank or Company: _____

= $ _____ Total

✏️ **This is Box 5.** Enter the total on Schedule B, Line 5 of your tax return. If this total is less than $1,500, you can just enter the amount on Form 1040, Line 9a.
   If the total is *more than* $1,500, also be sure to check the appropriate box(es) under Schedule B, Part III, Items 7 and 8.

Box 6: Figuring Self-Employment (Social Security) Tax for Ministers

Unless you're exempt from Social Security tax because you've filed Form 4361, you pay Social Security (self-employment) tax on your earnings as a minister. This tax applies to your salary, honorariums, other earned income *and* to your housing allowance.

Salary

- Enter your church salary on Schedule SE, Line 2 (this is the number from Box 1).

    Note: *Do not* enter your salary on Schedule SE if you have filed Form 4361 and are exempt from paying Social Security (self-employment) tax.

Line 21 Items

- If you have entered items on Form 1040, Line 21, and if you are not Social Security tax exempt, carry the total of the items from Line 21 to Schedule SE, Line 2.

    Important: Remember to subtract the total expenses on your Minister's Professional Expenses Worksheet (Box 7) from your Line 21 items before entering them on Schedule SE, Line 2.

    Note: *Do not* carry the amount(s) on Line 21 over to Schedule SE if you have filed Form 4361 and are exempt from paying Social Security (self-employment) tax.

    VERY Important: If you are a minister, and your W-2, Line 4 shows Social Security tax withheld (or if there are entries on your W-2, Lines 3, 5 or 6), your W-2 is incorrect and must be amended.

Housing Allowance

- If you are *not* Social Security tax exempt, enter your housing allowance on Schedule SE, Line 2 (long form).

    Important: Remember to subtract the total expenses on your Minister's Professional Expenses Worksheet (Box 7) from your housing before entering it on Schedule SE, Line 2.

    Note: *Do not* enter your housing allowance on Schedule SE if you have filed Form 4361 and are exempt from paying Social Security (self-employment) tax.

Parsonage

- If the church owns and provides a parsonage for you, enter the rental value of the parsonage plus the rental value of furnishings plus utilities on Schedule SE, Line 2 (long form).

    Important: Remember to subtract the total expenses on your Minister's Professional Expenses Worksheet (Box 7) from your parsonage amount before entering it on Schedule SE, Line 2.

    Note: *Do not* enter the rental value of your parsonage on Schedule SE if you have filed Form 4361 and are exempt from paying Social Security (self-employment) tax.

Rental Value of Your Parsonage

To find the rental value of your parsonage, answer the following question:

- About how much would the parsonage rent for per month if the church rented it out instead of letting you live there? (Consider factors such as church use of the parsonage, number of ministers occupying the parsonage, no choice in the matter of parsonage assigned, etc.)

    $_____

    Note: The Deason Rule does not apply on Schedule SE—*do not* reduce your business expenses by the percentage of your housing allowance. Subtract the full amount of your church-related business expenses on the following worksheet.

Worksheet to Figure Minister's Self-Employment (Social Security) Tax
(Clergy Tax Box 6)

$_____ **Salary**

$_____ **Form 1040, Line 21 Income Items**

$_____ **Schedule C Income**

$_____ **Housing Allowance**

$_____ **Fair Rental Value (FRV) of Parsonage**

= $_____ **Subtotal**

LESS

$_____ **Subtract the Total Amount of All Church-Related Business Expenses Paid out of Minister's Own Pocket and *Not* Reimbursed by the Church**

= $_____ **Total**

✎ **This is Box 6.** Enter the total on Schedule SE, Line 2 and attach this worksheet to your tax return.

Copyright © 2006 J. David Epstein, J.D. Permission to photocopy granted. *Clergy Tax 2007*

2006 Housing Allowance: Home Owned or Rented and Housing Allowance Received

How to Figure Your Correct Housing Allowance

Although the housing allowance is one of the best tax benefits available to ministers, it is also one of the most confusing to figure out. Plan on putting some effort into this section—in return you may reap big rewards at tax time.

The housing allowance is limited to the *least* of:

1. Housing Item 1—The amount designated as housing allowance;
2. Housing Item 2—The amount actually spent on housing expenses; or
3. Housing Item 3—The Fair Rental Value (FRV) of your home.

Note: The Fair Rental Value rule (or FRV) was overturned by a court in the Warren case decided in May of 2000. The court in that case appeared ready to declare the housing allowance unconstitutional, so the U.S. Congress acted and brought back the Fair Rental Value limit, and President Bush signed the bill into law. It has been my opinion, and still is, that the Tax Court correctly decided the Warren case, and the fair rental value rule should be thrown out. Perhaps some day it will be, but for now, the Fair Rental Value rule is the law.

Housing Items 1, 2 and 3

The following worksheets will help you figure Housing Items 1 through 3.

Housing Item 1 Worksheet

How much housing allowance did the church designate for you in 2006 in addition to your regular salary?

[A] $_____

Has your housing amount been designated in your church minutes book? If not, you need to be sure you have church minutes to designate all housing allowances *in advance* of when such allowances are paid out to any ministers.

Was your housing money actually paid to you (or was it at least paid by the church directly for housing items on your behalf)? If not, and the amount of housing money you actually got was different from what was designated for you, please put the actual amount paid to you here (include any money paid by the church directly for housing items on your behalf):

[B] $_____

Now compare the amounts in lines **[A]** and **[B]**—which is less? Write that amount here:

$_____

✎ **This is Housing Item 1.**

16 Clergy Tax 2007

Housing Item 2 Worksheet

Following is the most complete listing of allowable housing expenses we know of. It was compiled from Letter Rulings, Tax Court cases and actual audits. Please enter the amount of 2006 housing (or parsonage) expenses that you paid in Column 1. (If your church paid any of these for you, enter that amount in Column 2.)

Item	Column 1 (You Paid)	Column 2 (Church Paid)
Rent	$_____	$_____
Mortgage Payments	$_____	$_____
Down Payment	$_____	$_____
Insurance on Home and Contents	$_____	$_____
Real Estate Taxes	$_____	$_____
Maintenance, Pest Control, Etc.	$_____	$_____
Repairs, Plumbing, Electrical Work, Etc.	$_____	$_____
Kitchen Items (plates, silverware, dishes, utensils, cups, glasses, cookware, etc.)	$_____	$_____
Household Cleaning Supplies (soap, detergent, tissues, broom, lightbulbs, trash bags, etc.)		
Furniture and Furnishings (purchase, repair and upkeep)	$_____	$_____
Appliances (purchase, repair and upkeep)	$_____	$_____
Curtains, Rugs, Linens, Towels, Pictures, Frames, Decorating Items, Wallpaper, Door Locks, Etc.	$_____	$_____
Utilities (electricity, gas, telephone, sewer, water, trash pickup, cable TV, firewood)	$_____	$_____
Landscaping, Lawn Services, Gardening, Fencing	$_____	$_____
Adding On Rooms or Other Structural Changes	$_____	$_____
Other (but not food, servants or entertainment)	$_____	$_____
= **Totals**	$_____	$_____

✎ The total in Column 1 is Housing Item 2.

Housing Item 3 Worksheet

This worksheet will show you how to estimate the Fair Rental Value (FRV) of your home.

A. **How much do you think your home would sell for if you sold it today?**

$ _____

Multiply this number by .01.

[A] $ _____

Example: Let's say your home is worth $100,000; $100,000 X .01 = $1,000.

Note: Where there are church-related meetings in a parsonage, more than one minister living in the same parsonage, no choice in matter of the parsonage assigned or similar factors, the Fair Rental Value of the parsonage may be considerably less than the value arrived at by this formula.

B. **How much did you pay for your furniture?**

$ _____

Multiply this number by 3; then divide by 24.

[B] $ _____

Example: Let's say your furniture cost $8,000; $8,000 X 3 = $24,000.
$24,000 ÷ 24 = $1,000. **Note:** In some areas, multiply the furniture cost by 2 instead of 3.

C. **What is your estimated total utility bill each month?** (Be sure to include electricity, gas, telephone, sewer, water, trash pickup, cable TV, firewood, etc.)

[C] $ _____

D. **Now, add up [A] + [B] + [C] to get an estimate of the maximum amount of housing allowance you qualify for each month** (aka the FRV as referred to by the IRS).

[D] $ _____

✎ **This is Housing Item 3.**

Excess Housing Allowance (Housing Item 4)

Housing Item 4 Worksheet

Was any of the housing allowance you received not actually spent on housing items?

If no, stop here—you don't have excess housing allowance.
If yes, how much was not spent on housing?

$_____

✎ This amount goes on Form 1040, Line 21. Write "excess housing allowance" on the line.

✎ Also carry this amount to the last item on the W-2 Income Worksheet (page 8).

Hint: Here's how to figure how much of your housing allowance was not actually spent on housing expenses:

1. **Enter the number from Housing Item 1 here:**

   [A] $_____

   This is the amount the church designated and actually paid you for housing.

2. **Enter the number from Housing Item 2 here:**

   [B] $_____

   This is the amount you actually spent on housing. (Be sure to use only the total from Column 1.)

3. **Compare these two numbers**—Is [A] more than [B]? If yes, you have excess housing allowance. Subtract [B] from [A] and enter the result here:

   [A] − [B] = $_____

   ✎ This is the excess amount that goes on Form 1040, Line 21 according to the directions for Box 1 on page 9.

Example: If [A], the housing allowance the church paid you, is $20,000 and [B], the amount you actually spent on housing, is $15,000; then you just subtract [B] ($15,000) from [A] ($20,000), and you get the excess amount of $5,000. This amount goes on Form 1040, Line 21 according to the directions for Box 1.

Note: It is also possible, though unlikely, that you can have excess housing allowance because the FRV of your home is less than what you spent on housing items. Most often, this situation occurs when a minister adds a room or an addition to the home, makes a large down payment when buying a home, pays down the mortgage on a home significantly in a given year, and so on. If you have this situation, the church can arrange to pay these amounts over several years, in order to keep them within the FRV rule.

Important: The entire amount of housing allowance paid to you is subject to self-employment (Social Security) tax unless you are exempt from Social Security tax because you have filed Form 4361, or are retired.

If you *are* retired, and your church designates your housing allowance from your pension, then it should not be subject to Social Security (self-employment) tax on Schedule SE. This is so even though the Ministers' Audit Guidelines released by the IRS say that a retired minister's housing allowance *is* subject to SE tax. Congress acted a few years ago, and passed a law that says that retired ministers may now receive a housing allowance, and owe no Social Security tax on it. Utilities are also covered. (This benefit is retroactive and retired ministers who paid Social Security tax on their housing allowances in 2003, 2004 or 2005 may be able to file amended returns to claim a refund.)

Box 7: Minister's Professional Expenses

Did the church reimburse you for church-related expenses in 2006?

If no, photocopy and complete the reproducible "Supporting Schedule to Form 2106: Minister's Professional Expense Worksheet" on page 21.

If yes, has your church adopted an accountable church reimbursement policy in its minutes? If it has, fill out Box 7 *only for expenses for which the church has not reimbursed you*. **Note:** If your church has not adopted this policy in its minutes, you're missing out on a great tax benefit. See the next-to-last item in Box 1.

Only expenses which you paid for out of your own pocket, and for which you were *never reimbursed* by the church should be listed on Box 7's worksheet. (These expenses include seminars, conventions and so forth. It is best to keep a trip diary for your records, to show the ministry purpose of the travel.)

Once you've completed the worksheet, attach it to your tax return. (**Alternative:** If you do not want to use the worksheet as an attachment to your tax return, enter all the expenses—except meals and entertainment—on Form 2106, Line 4; then put the amount for meals and entertainment on Form 2106, Line 5).

Do you have receipts for your minister's professional expenses? If so, keep them in a separate folder marked "2006 Expenses." These items are often checked by an IRS agent when auditing a minister's tax return. If you do not have receipts for some items, they can still be deducted, but you should know that if your return is audited, they will probably be disallowed unless you kept an expense diary during the year. An expense diary can be as simple as a pocket calendar you use while traveling in which you write the expense, business purpose, and amount on the day you paid it. Use it for expenses under $75 for which you don't have receipts.

> **Note:** Be sure you get reimbursements for all church-related expenses—a recent federal case says if you could have been reimbursed, but did not choose to, you may lose the right to deduct the expenses on your personal tax return.

Supporting Schedule to Form 2106: Minister's Professional Expense Worksheet

(Clergy Tax Box 7)

Name of Minister: _____

Social Security Number: _____ - _____ - _____

Educational Expenses	$ _____
Business Telephone	$ _____
Office Supplies	$ _____
Postage	$ _____
Books	$ _____
Tapes	$ _____
Other Religious Materials	$ _____
Tax Return Preparation	$ _____
Seminars and Dues	$ _____
Subscriptions and Fees	$ _____
Office Equipment	$ _____
Post Office Box	$ _____
Legal and Accounting Fees and Expenses	$ _____
Supplies (including vestments and cleaning)	$ _____
Interest on Charge Cards Used for Business	$ _____
Interest on Auto Loans for Cars Used 100% for Business	$ _____
Business Meals, Entertainment, Tips X 50%	$ _____
Travel (auto rental, airfares, train fares, bus fares, hotel, laundry and cleaning, parking and tolls, telephone)	$ _____
Interest on Other Business-Related Loans (including credit union, finance company, personal, educational, bank or life insurance loans)	$ _____
= Total	$ _____

✎ **This is Box 7.** Enter the total on Form 2106, Line 4.

Copyright © 2006 J. David Epstein, J.D. Permission to photocopy granted. *Clergy Tax 2007*

2006 Itemized Deductions

Box 8: Medical Expenses

Please list the amount of any medical expenses you had in 2006 which were not reimbursed by the church and not paid for by the insurance company. In other words, these are amounts you paid for *out of your own pocket*.
Note: Items with an asterisk (*) must be related to a medical condition or prescribed by a doctor to be deductible.

Box 8 Worksheet

Insurance Premiums	$_____
Medicare Premiums	$_____
Prescriptions	$_____
Doctors	$_____
Dentists	$_____
Hospitals	$_____
Equipment (e.g., eyeglasses, dentures, hearing aids, special shoes, etc.)	$_____
Lab Fees	$_____
Nursing Costs	$_____
Medical Supplies	$_____
Air Conditioning*	$_____
Humidifier*	$_____
Electricity*	$_____
Transportation*	$_____
Hotel*	$_____
Mileage (at 18 cents per mile)	$_____
Other: _____	$_____
= Total	$_____

✎ **This is Box 8.** Enter the total on Schedule A, Line 1.

Box 9: Real Estate, Property and State Taxes

Box 9 Worksheet

A. **Real Estate Tax Paid on Your Home**

    [A] $_____

    ✎ Enter this amount on Schedule A, Line 6.

B. **Personal Property Tax Paid**

    [B] $_____

    ✎ Enter this amount on Schedule A, Line 7.

C. **Is there a number on either Line 17 or Line 19 of your W-2?** This is state or local tax that was withheld from your salary on your church or other W-2. Write the amount here:

    [C1] $_____

    Was there state tax you paid that was not included on your W-2? Write the amount here.
    (Check your 2005 state income-tax return. If you owed state income tax when you filed and sent in a check with your 2005 state return, write the amount here.)

    [C2] $_____

    Add: [C1] + [C2] = $_____

    ✎ Enter this amount on Schedule A, Line 5.

Box 10: Interest on Real Estate and Home Equity Loans

Box 10 Worksheet

Real Estate Mortgage Loan Interest Paid on Your Home	$_____
Home Equity Loan Interest Paid	$_____
Total	$_____

✎ **This is Box 10.** Enter the total on Schedule A, Line 10.

Worksheet for Church Autos

Annual Lease Value Worksheet

Fair Market Value of the Vehicle	$_____
Annual Lease Value (ALV) (See the Annual Lease Value Table, p. 26)	$_____
Amount of Gasoline Paid for by the Church During the Year	$_____
Add: **ALV + Gasoline Amount**	$_____
Amount (Percentage) **of Personal Use**	_____%
Multiply: **Total ALV + Gasoline Amount X Personal Use Percentage**	$_____

✎ Enter this total amount from the Annual Lease Value Worksheet on Line 5 of the W-2 Income Worksheet (page 8).

Many pastors use a church-owned vehicle—and if there is personal mileage allowed on a church-owned vehicle, then some amount should be included on the pastor's W-2 at the end of year. Here is how you figure the correct amount to show on a minister's W-2 for personal use of a church auto.

Scan the ALV Table located on page 24 and locate in column 1 the vehicle's Fair Market Value (FMV)—what you paid for the car if it was purchased less than 4 years ago. Once you find the correct FMV in the list, look across to the right in column 2 to find the corresponding Annual Lease Value (ALV).

Once you have located the auto's ALV, multiply the ALV times the percentage of personal use to find the amount that goes on the pastor's W-2.

If the church pays for gas, add 5.5 cents per mile to the W-2 for gas on personal miles. You can also use the actual cost of the gasoline, whichever you prefer. (You'll find that the more expensive the price of gasoline, and the less mileage the car gets, the more you will benefit from using the 5.5-cents-per-mile rule. For example, if your car gets 15 miles to a gallon, then 15 miles times 5.5 cents per mile = an effective rate of $.83 cents a gallon included on your W-2.)

> **Example:** Let's say the auto cost $15,000. You can see that the ALV for $15,000 is $4,350. Let's say that the pastor used the car 10% for personal use. The correct amount to put on the W-2 is $435, or $4,350 times 10%. You also have to add in gasoline. So let's say the church paid for $1,200 of gasoline during the year. Take $1,200 times 10% (the gasoline used for personal use) and you get $120. Add that to the use of the car, $435 + $120, and you get $555, the amount that goes on the W-2. (Or use the special 5.5-cents-per-mile-per-gallon rule above if it results in a lesser gasoline cost.) This amount is added both to the W-2, Line 14 and also to the amount of salary on Line 1. (Yes, that is correct: the same number is added both to Line 1 and to Line 14 of the W-2.) Let's say in W2, Line 1 there is $10,000 of salary, and that W2, Line 14 is blank. You add $555 to both Line 1 and Line 14—so now Line 1 will read $10,555, and Line 14 will read $555.

You can prorate the ALV if the church owned the car less than the full year, and you should figure out the Fair Market Value of the car again on January 1 after the 4th full calendar year the car has been used. Use this new fair market value figure to find the new ALV (which will now be lower).

You can also use a new Fair Market Value figure on January 1 of the year of transfer of a church auto from one staff person to another.

> **Example:** Let's say the church bought the car July 1, 2005, for $20,000. The ALV for each of the first 4 full years (2005 prorated, 2006, 2007, 2008 and 2009) would be $5,600. As of January 1, 2010, you would revalue the car at whatever it was worth on that date.
>
> Let's say on January 1, 2010, the car is worth $10,000. Then the new ALV would be $3,100 for the next 4 years, and so on.

Annual Lease Value Table

Fair Market Value $0–$21,999	Corresponding Annual Lease Value $	Fair Market Value $22,000 and Up	Corresponding Annual Lease Value $
0–999	600	22,000–22,999	6,100
1,000–1,999	850	23,000–23,999	6,350
2,000–2,999	1,100	24,000–24,999	6,600
3,000–3,999	1,350	25,000–25,999	6,850
4,000–4,999	1,600	26,000–27,999	7,250
5,000–5,999	1,850	28,000–29,999	7,750
6,000–6,999	2,100	30,000–31,999	8,250
7,000–7,999	2,350	32,000–33,999	8,750
8,000–8,999	2,600	34,000–35,999	9,250
9,000–9,999	2,850	36,000–37,999	9,750
10,000–10,999	3,100	38,000–39,999	10,250
11,000–11,999	3,350	40,000–41,999	10,750
12,000–12,999	3,600	42,000–43,999	11,250
13,000–13,999	3,850	44,000–45,999	11,750
14,000–14,999	4,100	46,000–47,999	12,250
15,000–15,999	4,350	48,000–49,999	12,750
16,000–16,999	4,600	50,000–51,999	13,250
17,000–17,999	4,850	52,000–53,999	13,750
18,000–18,999	5,100	54,000–55,999	14,250
19,000–19,999	5,350	56,000–57,999	14,750
20,000–20,999	5,600	58,000–59,999	15,250
21,000–21,999	5,850	60,000–up	.25 X Auto Fair Market Value + $500

Box 11: Business Auto Mileage

You can use Option 1 (your actual mileage) or Option 2 (your actual auto expenses) as a deduction for the business use of your vehicle.

Option 1—Mileage

What is the total number of miles you drove on church business in 2006?

_____ miles

✎ Enter this number on Form 2106, Part II, Line 13. (The mileage rate for 2006 is 44.5 cents per mile.)

Option 2—Expenses

To deduct your actual auto expenses instead of your mileage, use the following Auto Expenses Worksheet. Multiply the total auto expenses by the percentage of business use to find the amount you can deduct.

Auto Expenses Worksheet

Information	Auto 1	Enter on Form 2106	Auto 2	Enter on Form 2106
Year and Make	_____	n/a	_____	n/a
Date of Purchase	_____	Line 11a	_____	Line 11b
Purchase Price	$ _____	Line 30a	$ _____	Line 30b
Total Miles in 2006	_____	Line 12a	_____	Line 12b
Business Miles in 2006	_____	Line 13a	_____	Line 13b

Expenses	Auto 1	Auto 2
Gasoline	$_____	$_____
Insurance and Auto Club	$_____	$_____
License and Registration	$_____	$_____
Auto Excise and Sales Taxes	$_____	$_____
Parking and Tolls	$_____	$_____
Oil, Service and Repairs	$_____	$_____
Tires and Batteries	$_____	$_____
Washing and Waxing	$_____	$_____
= **Totals**	$_____	$_____

✎ Enter this total on Line 23a of Form 2106.*

✎ Enter this total on Line 23b of Form 2106.*

*__Note:__ If you are filing a Schedule C, these totals go on Schedule C, Line 9. Also remember to figure depreciation for your car(s) used for business on Schedule C, Line 13.

Do you have written receipts for these expenses? Do you have a mileage log to prove business mileage? If you don't have an auto log or written receipts, and if your return is audited, you can expect an IRS examiner to want proof of these expenses. That doesn't mean you can't deduct them, it just means that you could be asked to back up your auto expense deductions.

BOX 12: CHARITABLE CONTRIBUTIONS

Box 12 Worksheet

A. Cash Contributions to Your Church

$_____

✎ Enter this amount on Schedule A, Line 15.

Is the total amount of cash contributions to your church more than $1,000? If yes, you should probably attach to your return a copy of the letter your church sent you which verifies the total amount of your contributions for 2006. In addition, if you made one or more separate contributions of $250 or more to your church, you should be sure the church gives you a letter with your total contributions. (The IRS has responded to comments from churches that found it a hardship to keep records for every donation of $250 or more that came in. IRS Regulations have now been modified to state that, where a donor makes one or more $250 contributions in a given year to a church, one giving statement showing the *total amount* of the donor's contributions for the year will satisfy IRS rules.)

B. Cash Contributions to Other Ministries

$_____

✎ Enter this amount on Schedule A, Line 15.

C. Value of Noncash Contributions (clothing, supplies, furniture, jewelry, etc.)

$_____

✎ Enter this amount on Schedule A, Line 16.

Note: If the value is more than $500, you'll need to fill out and attach Form 8283 to your return (see IRS instructions).

D. Cash Contributions to Be Carried Over from Last Year

$_____

✎ Enter this amount on Schedule A, Line 17.

E. Cash Contributions to Be Carried Over to *Next Year*

$_____

✎ Make a record of this number; then enter this amount on Schedule A, Line 17 of your *2007* (next year's) tax return.

28 Clergy Tax 2007

PART TWO

ITEMS THAT MAY NOT APPLY TO ALL PASTORS

Many ministers do not have to deal with the areas in this section; to determine if you do, simply "ski" down the list, and as you go mark the box next to any item you think might apply to you. When you've scanned through the list, go back and—one item at a time—refer to the corresponding pages for any items you've checked. As a final step, go through the checklists beginning on page 41 of this section to make sure you didn't miss anything; then you're done—congratulations!

Reminder: If you need a tax form, you can call the IRS at 1-800-TAX-FORM to request it. You can also download any form you need directly from the IRS website at http://www.irs.ustreas.gov/formspubs/index.html and then select the "Form and Instruction number" link.

If Item Applies (during the 2006 tax year)   See Page

❑	Item 1	Did Not Receive a Form W-2	31
❑	Item 2	Had Personal Use of Church Vehicle	31
❑	Item 3	Need an Extension to File Your Tax Return	31
❑	Item 4	Received a Partnership, Estate or Corporation Form K-1	31
❑	Item 5	Received Pension Benefits or Annuities	32
❑	Item 6	Received Royalties	32
❑	Item 7	Rendered Babysitting Services and/or Had Other Odd Jobs	32
❑	Item 8	Received a State Income Tax Refund	32
❑	Item 9	Paid for Child Care While Working (includes payments to the church day-care center)	32
❑	Item 10	Received Social Security Payments	33
❑	Item 11	Received Child Support Payments	33
❑	Item 12	Received Alimony Payments	33
❑	Item 13	Traveled with Spouse and/or Children on Church Business at the Church's Expense	33
❑	Item 14	Purchased Personal Items (clothes, jewelry, furniture, electronics, etc.) Directly from Church Funds	33
❑	Item 15	Received Personal Funds Directly from Petty Cash or Church Offerings	33
❑	Item 16	Had Own Business (i.e., any work done on the side to earn extra money)	33
❑	Item 17	Had Investments in the Stock Market	33
❑	Item 18	Sold a Major Item for Cash or on an Installment Sale	33
❑	Item 19	Owned Rental Property and Received Rent from Tenants	33
❑	Item 20	Received Income from Bartering Goods and/or Services	33
❑	Item 21	Made a One-Time Gift Greater Than $12,000 to an Individual	34

- ❏ **Item 22** Had a Casualty or Theft Loss *Not* Covered by Insurance 34
- ❏ **Item 23** Had a Change in Marital Status 34
- ❏ **Item 24** Incurred Ministry-Related Educational Expenses 34
- ❏ **Item 25** Received Notices and/or Settled an IRS Audit 34
- ❏ **Item 26** Had Any of the Following Deductions 34
  - Alimony Paid
  - Contributions to Colleges or Universities
  - Donations to District Office of Minister's Denomination
  - Job-Hunting Expenses
  - Personal Property Tax
- ❏ **Item 27** Gave Any of the Following Items to Charity 35
  - Auto Mileage
  - Clothing
  - Coins
  - Furniture
  - Jewelry
  - Other Noncash Item
  - Other Travel Expenses
  - Real Estate
  - Supplies for Charity
- ❏ **Item 28** Made Contributions to an IRA or Other Pension Plan
  (includes spouse's contributions) 35
- ❏ **Item 29** Withdrew Funds from an IRA or Other Pension Plan 36
- ❏ **Item 30** Rolled Over Funds from One IRA or Other Pension Plan
  to Another 36
- ❏ **Item 31** Had Contributions Made by the Church for You to IRA
  or Other Pension Plan (e.g., 403(b) Plan) 36
- ❏ **Item 32** Received Paid Health-Related Expenses from the Church
  (including insurance premiums) *and* Received a Form 1099
  Instead of a Form W-2 36
- ❏ **Item 33** Refinanced a Home 37
- ❏ **Item 34** Moved from One Residence to Another 37
- ❏ **Item 35** Purchased or Sold a Home 37
- ❏ **Item 36** Sold Other Real Estate 37
- ❏ **Item 37** Had an Office in the Home Used Exclusively
  for Church Business 37
- ❏ **Item 38** Carried Over a Capital Loss from Last Year 38
- ❏ **Item 39** Received a Form 1099 from the Church 38
- ❏ **Item 40** *Did* Have Social Security Tax Withheld from Paycheck 39
- ❏ **Item 41** Did *Not* Have Income Tax Withheld from Paycheck 39
- ❏ **Item 42** Paid Estimated Tax Each Quarter 39
- ❏ **Item 43** Want $3 to go to the Presidential Election Campaign Fund 40
- ❏ **Item 44** Did *Not* File Income Tax Return Last Year 40
- ❏ **Item 45** Are *Not* Ordained or Licensed
  or Are Not Yet Social Security Tax Exempt 40
- ❏ **Item 46** Minister or Spouse Is Exempt from Social Security Tax
  (has filed a valid Form 4361) 40

❑	Item 47	Are Taking an Aggressive Tax-Return Position (or one in which the facts are not conclusive)	.41
❑	Item 48	Organize Receipts	.41
❑	Item 49	Had Any Other Income	.41
❑	Item 50	Had Social Security Matching	.41

Actions to Take for Marked Items

Item 1—No Form W-2 Received

✎ If you did not receive a W-2, you can use Form 4852 instead. Request the form from the IRS and fill in the blanks using the information from Box 1 (or from the Box 1 "W-2 Income Worksheet") for the amount that should have been on your W-2.

Item 2—Personal Use of Church Auto

If the church provided a car for you during 2006 (i.e., if the church owns your car, and you have personal use of the church auto),

- **Does the church have a written policy about church-owned cars in the church minutes?**
    If no, you need to write up minutes for this.
    If yes, did the church include any amount for personal use on your W-2 or 1099 because of the car?
        If yes, you don't need to use the "Church Auto Worksheet."
        If no, you need to include the personal use of the car on your tax return.
- **Did the church give you any other type of auto allowance in 2006?**
    If so, write the total amount here:

    $_____

✎ If you turned in a record of your miles and the church reimbursed you at 44.5 cents per mile, you don't have to report this as income; however, if the church just paid you a *cash auto allowance* and didn't ask you for any receipts, you must report the cash allowance as income.

If this cash auto allowance is not already on your W-2 or 1099, enter the total amount on Form 1040, Line 21. Under "Description," write in "Cash auto allowance." If you are *not* Social Security tax exempt, also enter this amount on Schedule SE, Line 2. (*Do not* carry this amount to Schedule SE if you have filed Form 4361 to be exempt from Social Security tax.)

Item 3—Filing Extensions

✎ If you can't file your tax return on or before April 16, 2007, you need to file an extension on Form 4868 until August 15, 2007. You will still have to pay your tax on April 16, 2007, even if you file an extension, but you will have more time to get your information together. If you can't file your tax return on or before the August 15, 2007, extension date, you can file a second extension on Form 2688 until October 15, 2007. (The second extension is not granted automatically, although the first one usually is.)

IMPORTANT! *Always* use certified mail (return-receipt requested) or FedEx to file any extension(s)! It is the only proof the IRS will accept.

Item 4—Partnership, Estate or Corporation Form K-1

✎ If you received a Partnership, Estate or Corporation Form K-1, enter these amounts on Form 1040 and accompanying Schedules according to the instructions you received with your K-1.

Item 5—Pension Benefits or Annuities

For distributions from Pensions, Annuities, Retirement Plans or IRAs you'll need the Form(s) 1099R you received:

Name of Bank or Company Amount

$_____ **Bank or Company:** _____

$_____ **Bank or Company:** _____

$_____ **Bank or Company:** _____

$_____ **Bank or Company:** _____

=$_____ **Total Distributions Received**

✎ Enter the total amount—*except IRA distributions*—on Form 1040, Line 16a. (Carry any taxable amount to Form 1040, Line 16b.)

✎ Enter IRA distributions on Form 1040, Line 15a. (Carry any taxable amount to Form 1040, Line 15b.)

Item 6—Royalties Received

List royalties received here:

$_____ **Company:** _____

$_____ **Company:** _____

$_____ **Company:** _____

$_____ **Company:** _____

=$_____ **Total Royalties Received**

✎ Enter the total on Schedule E, Line 4.

Item 7—Income from Babysitting or Other Odd Jobs

List miscellaneous income here:

$_____ **Babysitting**

$_____ **Odd Jobs**

$_____ **Source:** _____

=$_____ **Total Miscellaneous Income**

✎ Enter this amount on Form 1040, Line 21. (Also carry this amount to Schedule SE, Line 2 if you are *not* Social Security exempt or if the income was *not* ministry-related.)

Item 8—State Income Tax Refund

$_____ **State Income Tax Refund Received***

✎ Enter this amount on Form 1040, Line 10.

*You should check your income tax return for last year to see if you have to include this amount as income this year; a state income tax refund is income only under certain circumstances. If you couldn't deduct your state tax on last year's Schedule A, you may not have to include your state refund as income in 2006.

Item 9—Payments for Child Care Services

✎ If you paid anyone to care for your child(ren) so you could work in 2006, use Form 2441 for the Child Care Credit. **Note:** There is a new adoption credit. Use Form 8839 and follow IRS instructions.

Item 10—Social Security Payments

$_____ **Total Social Security Payments Received***

✎ Enter this amount on Form 1040, Line 20a. (Carry any taxable amount to Form 1040, Line 20b.)

*Sometimes these payments are nontaxable, and sometimes they are partially or fully taxable. Tax preparation software should figure this for you automatically.

Item 11—Child Support Payments

Child support payments are nontaxable and do not have to be reported on your tax return.

Item 12—Alimony Payments Received

$_____ **Total Alimony Received**

✎ Enter this amount on Form 1040, Line 11.

Item 13—Family Members' Travel at Church Expense

✎ If you, as a minister, have had your spouse or children travel with you on church business at the church's expense, the extra amounts spent for your spouse and children are taxable and should be reported on your W-2. If you have this type of income, and it's not on your W-2, enter it on Form 1040, Line 21 (and also on Schedule SE, Line 2 if you are *not* Social Security exempt). You only have to include the extra amount; for example, if your spouse stays in the same hotel room you would have had anyway, there is no extra income; but if he or she needs a separate plane ticket, this extra amount is reportable as income—*unless* your spouse works with you in the ministry and was with you on church business. In this case, the extra amounts for his or her travel do not have to be reported.

Item 14—Purchase of Personal Items with Church Funds

✎ If you purchased any personal items (such as clothes, jewelry, furniture, electronics, etc.) directly from church funds, these amounts are taxable, and should be reported as income on your W-2.

If you have this type of income, and it's not on your W-2, enter the amount on Form 1040, Line 21 (and also on Schedule SE, Line 2 if you are *not* Social Security exempt).

Item 15—Receipt of Personal Funds from Church Petty Cash or Church Offerings

✎ If you received personal funds directly from petty cash or from church offerings, these amounts are taxable, and should be reported as income on your W-2. If you have this type of income, and it's not on your W-2, enter the amount on Form 1040, Line 21 (and also on Schedule SE, Line 2 if you are *not* Social Security exempt).

Item 16—Separate Business Activity

✎ If you had your own business in 2006 (i.e., if you did anything on the side where you earned money), use Schedule C and attach it to your tax return.

✎ If you have an office in your home that you used exclusively for this business in 2006, use Form 8829 and attach it to Schedule C.

Item 17—Investments in the Stock Market

✎ If you had any investments in the stock market, use the Schedule D form for gains or losses.

Item 18—Sale of a Major Item for Cash or an Installment Sale

✎ If you sold any kind of major item for cash or on an installment sale (i.e., where the person you sold it to is making payments to you each month—this could be for a house, a car, a boat or other major item), you may have to use Form 6252.

Item 19—Rental Property Ownership and Rental Income

✎ If you owned any rental property and received rent from tenants, use Schedule E and attach it to your tax return.

Item 20—Bartering for Goods and/or Services

✎ If you received any income from bartering goods or services, list this income on Form 1040, Line 21. (In some cases, you may need to carry this amount to Schedule SE, Line 2 if you are *not* Social Security exempt.)

Item 21—One-Time Gift Greater Than $12,000 to an Individual

✎ If you made a gift over the amount of $12,000 to an individual in 2006, you probably need to file a Form 709 gift tax return.

Item 22—Casualty and/or Theft Losses

✎ If you had casualty or theft losses, which were not covered by insurance, use Form 4684.

Item 23—Change in Marital Status

✎ If your marital status changed in 2006, indicate the date you were married, divorced or widowed here and see the instructions for IRS Form 1040: _____

Item 24—Ministry-Related Educational Expenses

✎ If you incurred educational expenses in 2006 to help you do your job better, you may be able to deduct them on Form 2106, Line 4—*unless the church paid for them.*

If the church paid these expenses, church-provided educational assistance will be tax-free up to $5,250 for 2006. (Congress originally extended this benefit through December 31, 2001, but it is now permanent through 2010 under the Bush tax plan. This tax break applied to graduate courses beginning January 1, 2002.)

Item 25—IRS Notices or Settlements

If you received notices or settled any IRS audits, are you using any changes agreed to for your audited return on this year's return? If not, these items are likely to be challenged again. On the other hand, if you have been audited for the past two years with no changes to your return, you shouldn't be audited again for a while. (If you are audited again, discuss the matter with a tax attorney or Certified Public Accountant, or ask to speak with the IRS Agent's Group Manager.)

Item 26—Donations, Property Tax, Alimony and/or Job Hunting Expenses

Alimony Paid

✎ Enter the total amount on Form 1040, Line 31a.

Contributions Made to Colleges and/or Universities

✎ Enter the total amount on Schedule A, Line 15.

Donations to Your Denomination's District Office (or whatever they call it)

✎ True charitable donations to your church, which are given for the sole reason that you want to give them, can only be deducted on Schedule A.

Note: There is a court case that says that if you are expected to make donations or tithe to your denomination in order to remain in good standing as a minister, you can deduct these expenses both on Schedule A and on Schedule SE if you get a W-2 (or, if you get a 1099, on Schedule C). You can expect, however, for the IRS to ask questions about whether you really are under a duty to make these contributions.

Job Hunting Expenses

✎ Enter the total amount on Schedule A, Line 20.

Personal Property Tax

✎ Enter the total amount on Schedule A, Line 7.

Item 27—Noncash Charitable Contributions

Use the following worksheet to determine the total noncash contributions you made in 2006.

_____ **Miles Driven**

$_____ **Total Auto Mileage** (miles driven X 14 cents per mile) (The special standard mileage rate in effect for 2006 for the cost of operating your car for providing charitable services solely related to Hurricane Katrina is 32 cents per mile.)

$_____ **Clothing**

$_____ **Coins**

$_____ **Furniture**

$_____ **Jewelry**

$_____ **Other Noncash Item:** _____

$_____ **Other Travel Expenses:** _____

$_____ **Real Estate**

$_____ **Supplies for Charity**

=$_____ **Total Noncash Contributions**

✎ Enter the total on Schedule A, Line 16.

✎ If the total of your noncash donations in 2006 was more than $500, please fill out Form 8283 (see the IRS instructions for this form).

Item 28—Contributions to an IRA or Other Pension Plan

IRA Contributions

✎ If you or your spouse made any contributions to an IRA in 2006, these IRA contributions should be entered on Form 1040, Line 32.

Other Pension Plan Contributions

If you as a minister or your church made contributions to a church pension plan (403[b] Plan), these amounts do not have to be reported on your tax return unless the minister or the church made more than the maximum contribution allowable. Contributions to a Section 403(b) church retirement plan by a minister are shown on Line 12 Code E of the minister's Form W-2, even though this amount is not taxable. Church contributions may be reported on the minister's W-2, Line 14.

Item 29—Withdrawals from an IRA or Other Pension Plan

IRA Withdrawals

✎ If you or your spouse made any withdrawals from an IRA in 2006, enter the total amount on Form 1040, Line 15a. (Carry any taxable portion to Line 15b.)

Other Pension Plan Withdrawals

✎ If you or your spouse made any withdrawals from a pension plan other than an IRA, enter the total amount on Form 1040, Line 16a. (Carry any taxable portion to Line 16b.)

Item 30—Rollovers from IRA or Other Pension Plans

IRA Rollovers

✎ If you made any rollovers from one IRA to another in 2006, enter the total amount on Form 1040, Line 15a. (Unless these were taxable for some reason, Line 15b will be zero.)

Pension Plan Rollovers

✎ If you made any non-IRA pension plan rollovers in 2006, enter the total amount on Form 1040, Line 16a. (Unless these were taxable for some reason, Line 16b will be zero.)

Item 31—Church-Paid IRA or Other Pension Plan Contributions

If the church made any contributions to a pension plan (such as a 403[b] Plan) for you in 2006, you don't have to report these on your tax return, unless the church made more than the maximum contribution allowable.

✎ If the church, however, made contributions directly to an IRA which you own, these contributions are taxable and should be shown on your W-2. (If the contributions were not reported on the W-2, they should be entered on Form 1040, Line 21; they can then be deducted on Form 1040, Line 32, subject to the standard IRA limits.)

Item 32—Church-Paid Health-Insurance Premiums and Receipt of a Form 1099

✎ If the church paid any health-insurance premiums for you in 2006, these are tax-free as long as you get a W-2 and not a 1099 from your church. If the church paid your health insurance premiums and issued to you a 1099 for your church salary instead of a W-2, report the total amount paid by the church on Schedule C, Line 1.

Note: Has your church adopted a church health-expense policy in the minutes? If the church is going to pay your health-insurance premiums, or reimburse you as a minister for your out-of-pocket health-related expenses, it is important that you have a written health-expense policy in the church minutes.

Tip: For 2006, the maximum health savings account (HSA) deduction has increased to $5,450 for family coverage.

Item 33—Home Refinanced

If you refinanced your home, please see IRS Form 1040 instructions for how to handle points and other possible deductions. The following worksheet will help you assemble the information you'll need:

```
  $_____    Loan Amount

  $_____    Cost of Regular Housing Items

  $_____    Cost of Any Improvements

  $_____    Proceeds Used for Education

  $_____    Proceeds Used for Medical Expenses

  $_____    Amount of Points

 =$_____    Total Refinance Amount
```

Note: If you paid the points for the refinance by separate check, be sure to keep a record of it, since it might not show up on your closing statement. It is not necessary anymore to pay by separate check in order to deduct points, since the bank should list them on your Form 1098.

Item 34—Moving Expenses

If you moved in 2006, use Form 3903.

Item 35—Sale or Purchase of a Home

If you bought or sold your home in 2006, use the new IRS Home Sale Worksheets and report any gain on Schedule D or Form 6252 (see IRS instructions in Publication 523). **Note:** Please review a copy of your closing statement(s), because it will often have listings of deductible taxes, interest (and possibly other items).

Did You Know? Under new laws now in effect, many people will not have to pay any capital gains tax when they sell their home.

Item 36—Sale of Other Real Estate

If you sold real estate *other than your personal residence* in 2006, use Schedule D (see IRS instructions).

Item 37—Home Office Used Exclusively for Church Business

If you have an office in your home that you used exclusively for church business in 2006, do you use this home office for church-related work that you cannot do at your regular church office because you don't have a regular church office, or for some other reason? If yes, answer the following questions:

- **Do you travel daily between this home office and the main church office? If so, what is the approximate mileage between your home office and the church office?**

  _____ miles

- **What is the approximate square footage in your house?**

  _____ sq. ft.

- **What is the approximate square footage of your home office?**

  _____ sq. ft.

> **Note:** If you spent more money on housing expenses than the church gave you for housing, you may be able to deduct some of the money you spent because you have a home office. Just know that the IRS looks at this area closely.
>
> If you can deduct these expenses, enter them on Schedule C, Line 30; then fill out your home office expenses on Form 8829 and attach it to your return.

Tips

- See IRS Publication 587 for a worksheet on figuring the home-office deduction.
- Even if you can't deduct expenses for a home office (e.g., because you also have an office at the church and there is no compelling reason for you to have an office at home other than personal convenience), you still may be able to deduct your auto mileage from your home office to your church office. (However, this still does not mean that you can deduct your home office expenses.)
- If you have a computer in your home office, be sure you can show that you use it for church business, and that the church allows you to keep it at home because they get more work out of you that way. If you can't show this, expect the IRS to ask you for a log of your computer use, which they will use to try to disallow any personal use of the computer. One way around this problem is for the church to require and make an entry in the church minute book that says that the church—not you—owns the computer and that the computer may not be used for personal use.
- Due to a tax law that went into effect beginning January 1, 1999, a minister now qualifies for a home office deduction if the following two criteria are met:

  1. The office is used by the minister to conduct administrative or management activities of a church or ministry, and
  2. There is no other fixed location where the minister conducts substantial administrative or management activities of the church or ministry.

As under prior law, deductions will be allowed for a home office meeting the above two-part test only if the office is exclusively used on a regular basis for church or ministry business by the minister and, in the case of a minister who is an employee, only if such exclusive use is for the convenience of the church.

Item 38—Capital Loss Carryover

✎ If you had a capital loss carryover from last year, enter the amount carried over on Schedule D, either on Line 6 or Line 14—whichever applies.

Item 39—Receipt of a Church-Issued Form 1099

If you received a church 1099 for 2006, be sure to read the information about 1099s in appendix 4 carefully. Typically you do not need to attach a 1099 to your tax return unless it shows that income tax was withheld from the money you received.

✎ Enter the number from the 1099, Line 7 on Schedule C, Line 1.

> **Note:** Sometimes a church will issue a W-2 to a minister for regular salary and also issue a 1099 for other income, such as a love offering, honorariums, etc. In cases like this where the only entry on a Schedule C would be the income, and there are no expenses to be deducted against that income (perhaps because the church has an accountable reimbursement plan), then there is no reason not to show the W-2

income on Form 1040, Line 7, and the 1099 income on Form 1040, Line 21.

Even if you have expenses to deduct, you can still use Form 1040, Line 21 for your 1099 income. You then deduct your expenses from your Schedule SE income (if you're not 4361 exempt) and take the 2 percent hit on Schedule A by deducting the expenses there instead of on schedule C. You will lower your audit risk by as much as 5 times at a total cost of the 2 percent difference on Schedule A. (Even if the IRS challenges this approach—which is highly unlikely—it will only work in your favor, since you will then pick up the 2 percent difference.) Some accountants won't like what I just said, but remember: The only person more boring than an accountant is an economist. And what do you get when you cross an economist with the godfather? An offer you can't understand!

In addition, the Form 1099 amount should be reported on Schedule SE (long form) *only if* the minister is *not* Social Security exempt.

ITEM 40—SOCIAL SECURITY TAX WITHHELD FROM MINISTER'S PAYCHECK

✎ If the church withheld Social Security or Medicare taxes from your paycheck on your W-2, Line 4 or 6, your W-2 is incorrect and should be corrected (you can do so by having your church file Form W-2c). **Note:** It is also incorrect to show Social Security or Medicare wages on Lines 3 or 5 of a minister's W-2.

ITEM 41—NO INCOME TAX WITHHELD FROM MINISTER'S PAYCHECK

If the church did not withhold income tax from your paycheck, it is okay, because ministers are exempt from income tax withholding. However, it is usually best to be on voluntary withholding, so you don't owe tax at the end of the year. If you don't have voluntary withholding, you should be paying in estimated tax each quarter.

ITEM 42—ESTIMATED QUARTERLY TAX PAYMENTS

If you paid estimated tax in 2006, write down how much you paid each quarter as indicated. (Please note that if you did not pay enough tax during the year, you will owe an underpayment penalty.)

Note: Do not include amounts paid with your 2005 tax return (filed 4/17/2006) or amounts paid in response to an IRS notice. Check carefully and record only amounts paid toward your 2006 income tax.

Tax Period	Date Due	Federal Tax Amount Paid	Date Paid	State Tax Amount Paid	Date Paid
1st Quarter	4/17/2006	$_____	_____	$_____	_____
2nd Quarter	6/15/2006	$_____	_____	$_____	_____
3rd Quarter	9/15/2006	$_____	_____	$_____	_____
4th Quarter	1/15/2007	$_____	_____	$_____	_____

✎ Enter your total estimated *federal* tax payments on Form 1040, Line 65.
✎ Is there any refund from your 2005 return that should carry over and be applied to this year's taxes? If so, enter it on Form 1040, line 65.
✎ Enter total estimated state tax payments on Schedule A, Line 5. (The deduction available in 2005 for state and local general sales taxes has expired and will not apply for 2006.)

Also, don't overlook payments you may have made if you filed an extension(s) for your return:

- **Form 4868 Extension**
  Enter the amount of any tax you sent in with your first extension here:

  $_____

✎ Enter extension payments on Form 1040, Line 69.

- **Form 2688 Extension**
  Enter the amount of any tax you sent in with your second extension here:

  $_____

✎ Enter extension payments on Form 1040, Line 69.

Item 43—Presidential Election Campaign Fund

✎ If you (or your spouse) want $3 to go to the Presidential Election Campaign Fund, check the box(es) near the top of Form 1040, Page 1, under your Social Security number(s) on the right.

Item 44—No Income Tax Return Filed

✎ If you did not file an income-tax return last year and you had income above the threshold for filing a return, you should *consult a competent tax professional immediately*.

Item 45—Nonordained or Unlicensed Ministers (or Those Not Yet Social Security Tax Exempt)

If you are not ordained or licensed as a minister, you cannot exclude housing allowance, and you must have income tax and Social Security tax (FICA) withheld from your paycheck.

If you *are* ordained, write the date you were ordained here:

_____

and the name of the ordaining church or ministry here:

_____

What was the first year you were paid for services as a minister?

_____

If the answer is 2005, 2006 or 2007, you can still qualify to file an exemption from Social Security tax—however, if you answered 2005, you only have until April 16, 2007, to file the exemption. (**Note:** Filing a valid extension on Form 4868 will extend your time to file the exemption to August 15, 2007, and then filing Form 2688 may extend the date to October 15, 2007; but this isn't guaranteed, since this second extension isn't automatically granted.)

> **IMPORTANT!** *Always* use certified mail (return-receipt requested) or FedEx to file extensions! It is the only proof of filing the IRS will accept.

If the date you were ordained is any other previous year and the *second year* you were paid for services as a minister is 2005, 2006 or 2007, you may still qualify to file the exemption from Social Security tax, assuming you meet all the other requirements. (You may also be able to file this exemption if you changed churches in 2005, 2006 or 2007, were reordained or have had a change of religious belief about receiving Social Security benefits on your earnings as a minister.)

Item 46—Exemption from Social Security Tax

Minister Is Exempt

✎ If you are exempt from Social Security tax (i.e., if you have ever filed Form 4361—Minister's Exemption from Social Security Tax), be sure to keep a copy of your approval(s) from the IRS in a safe place, and keep extra copies in other locations where you can find them if an auditor should ever want to see your approved copy. Then, be sure to write "Exempt—Form 4361" on the dotted line on Form 1040, Line 58.

Spouse Is Exempt

✎ If your spouse has ever filed Form 4361 to claim Social Security tax exemption, be sure to keep a copy of his or her approval(s) from the IRS in a safe place, and keep extra copies in other locations where you can find them if an auditor should ever want to see the approved copy. Then, be sure to write "Exempt—Form 4361" on the dotted line on Form 1040, Line 58.

Note: Any nonministry-related (i.e., secular) income continues to be subject to Social Security taxes.

Item 47—Aggressive Tax Return Position

If you are taking a tax return position that is aggressive, or one in which the facts are not conclusive, you should fully disclose the facts and your position using a separate piece of paper attached to your tax return. This can lower your audit risk, and may head off penalties if you are later questioned by the IRS on this item.

Item 48—Organize Receipts

Now, while it is fresh in your mind, is a good time to organize your receipts in a way that lines up with your tax return. This will eliminate trying to remember what went where if you want to review these items later.

Item 49—Other Income

✎ If you had any other income that has not been described as yet in this book, note it here, and then refer to the IRS instructions for how to handle reporting it.

$ _____ Source: _____

$ _____ Source: _____

$ _____ Source: _____

= $ _____ **Total Other Income**

Item 50—Social Security Matching

Churches are not supposed to match FICA for ministers. It is income to the minister if this happens.

The church pays a 7.65 percent share of FICA and Medicare taxes for *nonminister* employees only (this is the amount the church "matches" for a nonminister; it is not part of the employee's wages). If the church has matched FICA and Medicare tax on your W-2 as a minister, your church needs to amend your W-2 (sometimes this can result in a refund).

Final Checklists

Check Your Return

❏ Are your filing status and dependents shown correctly?

❏ Is your personal information shown correctly?

❏ Have you made a comparison of your 2006 return to your 2005 return to see if there are any unusual year-to-year changes in income, deductions or other items? (If you note any unusual changes, you'll want to examine the items in question for possible errors.)

❏ Do all the supporting schedules attached to your return tie in to the proper line on the first two pages of Form 1040?

❏ Are there copies of forms or schedules from your federal return that need to be attached to your state tax return? (Some states require you to attach certain federal forms or schedules to your state return for their information. Check in the instructions for your state return to find out which, if any, you need to copy and send with your state return.)

❏ Is there any refund from 2005 that should carry over and be applied to this year's taxes? (If so, enter it on Form 1040, line 65.)

❏ Is there any refund that should carry over from 2006 and be applied to your 2007 taxes? (If so, write that amount here for reference: $ _____.)

❏ If you are not on voluntary withholding, have you filled out a Form 1040-ES to show your estimated tax payments for 2007?

❏ Do you have any further questions about your return? If so, call the IRS help line at 1-800-829-1040 and then curl up in your favorite chair with a good book while you wait for someone to answer the phone.

When You Are Certain Your Return Is Accurate

- ❏ Sign and date your return—if you are married, have your spouse sign and date it too.
- ❏ Make a copy of your completed returns (federal and state), including all attachments.
- ❏ Make a copy of your W-2.
- ❏ Create a new file folder marked "2006 Tax Return and Records" and place your copies in the file.
- ❏ Staple your W-2(s) to the front of your return. (You don't need to attach 1099s to your return unless a 1099 shows Federal Income Tax withheld on Line 4 of the 1099.)
- ❏ If you owe any tax, staple a check (payable to "Internal Revenue Service" or "United States Treasury") to the front of your return.

If You Can't Pay What You Owe

VERY IMPORTANT: If you can't pay the tax you owe with your return, *file your return anyway*. This can help stop some penalties from accruing; if you can pay at least some of the tax you owe when you file, this will help stop other penalties from accruing.

After you file your return, you may have up to 60 days before the IRS computer gets around to billing you for the balance you owe. Send them a check for whatever amount you can afford to pay at that time. They often keep sending bills for up to 90 days before they begin taking serious enforcement actions. If you keep paying on your tax bill every time you get an IRS notice, you may be able to pay it off before something bad happens. **Note:** If you still can't pay the tax due, file Form 9465 to request installment payments (you can also file this form with your tax return if you wish).

Methods the IRS Will Accept as Proof of Mailing

The IRS will only accept the following as proof that you have filed your tax return. Use one of these methods just in case the return gets lost and you have to prove that you actually sent it. (Whichever method you choose, be sure to attach the receipt to your file copy of your return.)

United States Post Office
- Certified Mail (use the return-receipt-requested service)

Federal Express
- FedEx Priority Overnight
- FedEx Standard Overnight
- FedEx 2Day

Airborne Express
- Overnight Air Express Service
- Next Afternoon Service
- Second Day Service

United Parcel Service
- UPS Next Day Air
- UPS Next Day Air Saver
- UPS 2nd Day Air
- UPS 2nd Day Air A.M.

DHL Worldwide Express
- DHL Same Day Service
- DHL USA Overnight

Note: If your return is fairly thick because you have a lot of schedules and attachments, use a 9"x12" manila envelope so that you won't have to fold the return.

APPENDIX ONE

CHECKLISTS OF DEDUCTIONS FOR MINISTERS

Use the checklists in this appendix to make sure you haven't missed any of the common deductions for ministers.

PROFESSIONAL EXPENSES

You can only deduct the professional expenses for which your church has not reimbursed you, unless the church included these reimbursements on your W-2. If the reimbursements are included in your W-2, you can deduct the expenses on your return.

❑ Accounting Fees $_____

❑ Auto Expenses $_____

❑ Books $_____

❑ Business Telephone $_____

❑ Educational Expenses $_____

❑ Interest on Charge Cards Used for Business $_____

❑ Interest on Auto Loan(s) for
Vehicles Used 100% for Business $_____

❑ Interest on Other Business-Related Loan(s)
(e.g., loans from a credit union, bank, finance company;
personal, educational or life-insurance loans) $_____

❑ Office Equipment $_____

❑ Office Supplies $_____

☐ Other Religious Materials	$_____
☐ Post Office Box	$_____
☐ Postage	$_____
☐ Seminars and Dues	$_____
☐ Subscriptions and Fees	$_____
☐ Tapes	$_____
☐ Tax-Return Preparation	$_____
☐ Other: _____	$_____

Note: Did the church reimburse you for any of these church-related expenses? If yes, then deduct only the expenses for which your church has not reimbursed you. If your church has adopted an Accountable Church Reimbursement Policy in its minutes, the church should not put the reimbursements on your W-2, and you cannot deduct reimbursements on your tax return.

PROFESSIONAL TRAVEL

Professional travel includes seminars, conventions and the like. You can deduct items *not* paid for by the church. It is best to keep a trip diary for your records, to show the ministry purpose of the travel.

☐ Auto Rental	$_____
☐ Fares (air, train or bus)	$_____
☐ Hotel	$_____
☐ Laundry and Cleaning	$_____
☐ Meals	$_____
☐ Parking and Tolls	$_____
☐ Telephone	$_____

❑ Tips	$_____
❑ Other: _____	$_____

Important: The IRS almost always checks these types of expenses in an audit. Be sure you have receipts for your travel expenses, and keep the receipts in a separate file marked "2006 Travel Expenses." Note which items you don't have receipts for—these can still be deducted; but be warned that if your tax return is audited, they will probably be disallowed—unless you keep an expense diary during the year. This can be as simple as a pocket calendar in which you note each expense under $75 for which you don't have a receipt. Be sure to include the date and the business purpose of the expense. Also keep in mind that the church can reimburse you for all church-related expenses—including travel items—as a tax-free fringe benefit.

INCOME

Use the following checklist to help you account for all sources of income:

❑ **Babysitting**	$_____
❑ **Church Salary**	$_____
❑ **Honorariums**	$_____
❑ **Odd Jobs**	$_____
❑ **Sideline Business**	$_____
❑ **Taxable Fringe Benefits**	$_____

MISCELLANEOUS EXPENSES

The checklist in this section lists miscellaneous expenses you can deduct if they are church related or if you (or your spouse) have a sideline business. Please list every possible expense you can think of—every time you write down an expense, your tax bill goes down.

❑ **Accounting Fees**	$_____
❑ **Advertising and Promotion**	$_____
❑ **Appraisal Costs**	$_____
❑ **Auto and Truck Expenses**	$_____

- ❏ Bad Debts $_____

- ❏ Bank Service Charges $_____

- ❏ Business Club Expenses $_____

- ❏ Business Gifts $_____

- ❏ Business License and Regulatory Fees $_____

- ❏ Business Services $_____

- ❏ Business Taxes $_____

- ❏ Carrying Forward of Losses from Past Years $_____

- ❏ Cleaning and Care of Business Areas $_____

- ❏ Commissions $_____

- ❏ Consulting Fees $_____

- ❏ Contract Labor Paid $_____

- ❏ Convention Expenses $_____

- ❏ Depletion $_____

- ❏ Discounts Allowed Customers $_____

- ❏ Donations $_____

- ❏ Dues and Publications $_____

- ❏ Educational Expense to Maintain or Improve Present Skills $_____

- ❏ Employee Benefits and Programs $_____

- ❑ **Employee Medical Expenses** $_____

- ❑ **Equipment Rental** $_____

- ❑ **Freight and Shipping** $_____

- ❑ **Insurance** $_____

- ❑ **Interest: Finance Charges, Etc.** $_____

- ❑ **Interest: Mortgage** $_____

- ❑ **Janitorial Service** $_____

- ❑ **Keogh Plan Contributions** $_____

- ❑ **Laundry and Cleaning** $_____

- ❑ **Legal and Professional Fees** $_____

- ❑ **Library Expenses** $_____

- ❑ **Meals and Entertainment** (x 50%) $_____

- ❑ **Moving Costs** $_____

- ❑ **Obsolescence of Business Assets** $_____

- ❑ **Office Expense** $_____

- ❑ **Organizational Expenses** $_____

- ❑ **Pension and Profit-Sharing Plans and Contributions** $_____

- ❑ **Postage** $_____

- ❑ **Professional Journals** $_____

- ❏ **Purchases During the Year** $_____
- ❏ **Sales Returns, Refunds, Rebates or Allowances** $_____
- ❏ **Rent on Business Property** $_____
- ❏ **Repairs** $_____
- ❏ **Safe Deposit Box** $_____
- ❏ **Security and Guard Services** $_____
- ❏ **Service or Maintenance Contracts** $_____
- ❏ **Start-Up Expenses** $_____
- ❏ **Storage Fees** $_____
- ❏ **Stationery** $_____
- ❏ **Supplies and Materials** $_____
- ❏ **Tax: FICA and Unemployment Tax Paid for Employees** $_____
- ❏ **Tax: Real Estate** $_____
- ❏ **Tax: Personal Property** $_____
- ❏ **Tax: Sales** $_____
- ❏ **Telephone** $_____
- ❏ **Theft and Casualty Losses** $_____
- ❏ **Tools** $_____
- ❏ **Trash Collection** $_____

- ❏ Travel $_____

- ❏ Uniforms $_____

- ❏ Utilities $_____

- ❏ Wages Paid to Empoyees $_____

- ❏ Wages Paid to Spouse $_____

- ❏ Wages Paid to Children $_____

- ❏ Miscellaneous:

  _____ $_____

  _____ $_____

  _____ $_____

  _____ $_____

  _____ $_____

HOME OFFICE FOR SIDELINE BUSINESS

If you had a sideline business and had an office in your home for this business, this section applies to you.

Date Home Was Purchased _____

Total Square Footage of Home _____ sq. ft.

Square Footage Used for Business _____ sq. ft.

Purchase Price of Home (if applicable) $_____

Cost of Any Improvements Made $_____

Rent (if applicable) $_____

Interest (if applicable) $_____

Taxes (if applicable) $_____

Insurance $_____

Utilities $_____

Repairs Made for Personal Use of Home $_____

Repairs Made Exclusively for Business Use of Home $_____

APPENDIX TWO

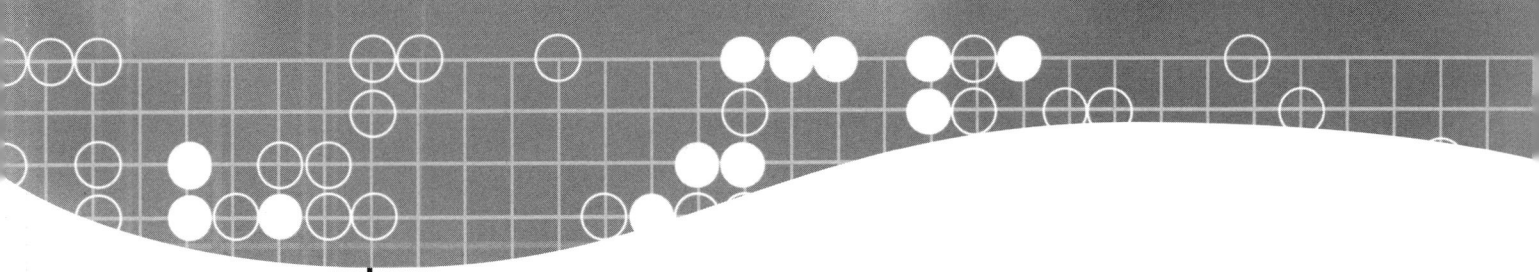

STATE FILING REQUIREMENTS

If your state requires you to file an income-tax return, you can probably carry over much of the information you've already gathered for your federal return. Several tax preparation software programs can carry over this information automatically to your State return.

Following is some additional information you may need:

- **What is the name of your school district?**

  _____

- **Do you work in a different county from the one in which you live? If yes, what is the name of the county in which you work?**

  _____

STATE TAX CREDITS

If your state has a rent credit, you'll need the following information:

- **For how many months total did you pay rent in 2006?**

  _____ months

- **What was your monthly rent during 2006?**

  $ _____ per month

- **What is your landlord's name and address?**

  _____

  _____

  _____

State tax credits can differ from federal ones (some are even more generous). Tax-preparation software can help you identify these credits more easily. If you don't have the means to fill out your state tax return using electronic software, and need to fill it out by hand, contact your State Revenue Office and request a complete package of blank 2006 Income Tax Forms for your state. The package will contain information specific to your state's filing requirements, and will have information regarding your state's tax credits. Be alert for State credits such as:

- ❏ Credit for Federal Income Tax Paid
- ❏ Credit for Federal Social Security Tax Paid
- ❏ Donation of Computers to Schools
- ❏ Educational or Job-Training Expense Credit
- ❏ Property Tax Paid
- ❏ School Tuition Credit
- ❏ Various Environmental and Wildlife Credits
- ❏ Other Types of Contribution Credits

Federal Forms and Schedules

Check the filing instructions for your state to find out if you need to attach any copies of the Forms or Schedules from your federal tax return to your State return. Many states require that you attach only certain Forms and Schedules; others require that you attach all of the Forms and Schedules (if this is the case, the State return form itself will often state that the Federal return must be attached).

APPENDIX THREE

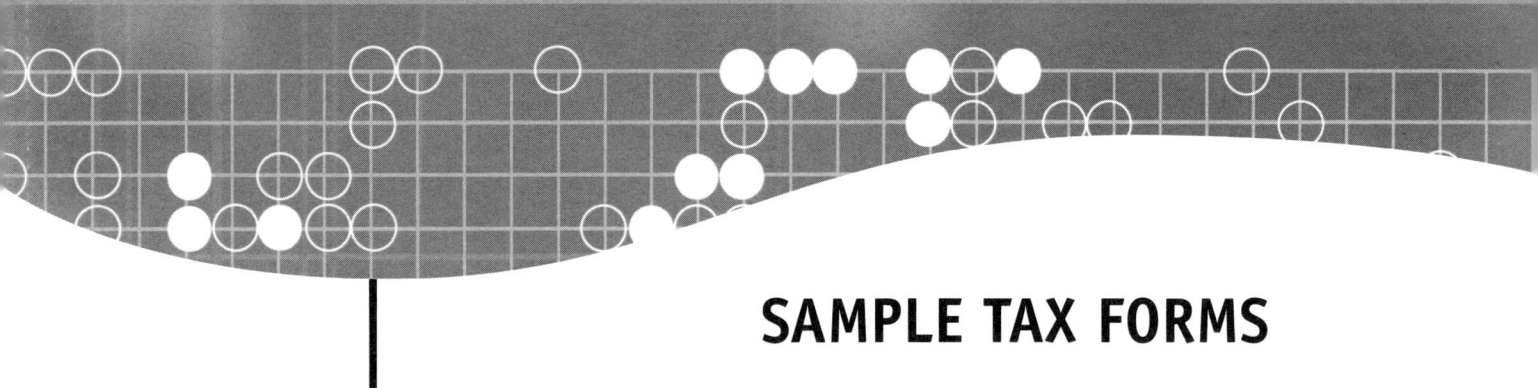

SAMPLE TAX FORMS

In this section you'll find the following sample tax Forms:

- W-2
- Form 1040
- Schedule A
- Schedule B
- Schedule SE

*If a Form Key goes to a Form that is not in these sample forms, that means that the form isn't used very much by ministers. To get any of these kinds of forms, simply go to http://www.irs.ustreas.gov/formspubs/lists/0,,id=97817,00.html where the IRS has downloads for every form you might possibly need.

Please Note: The sample forms in this appendix are provided for informational use only. Do not reproduce and use them for your tax return because the IRS wants you to use their forms. If you do not have all of the forms you need to file your return, you can request the forms by calling 1-800-TAX-FORM or you can download them directly from the IRS website at http://www.irs.ustreas.gov/formspubs/index.html. Select the "Form and Instruction number" link to find the form you need.

AN IMPORTANT NOTE FROM THE IRS

"[The sample forms in this appendix are] advance proof [copies] of IRS tax [forms]. They are subject to change and OMB approval before [they are] officially released. You can check the scheduled release date on our web site (www.irs.gov).

If you have any comments on [these] draft [forms], you can submit them to us on our web site. Include the word "draft" in your response. You may make comments anonymously, or you may include your name and e-mail address or phone number. We will be unable to respond to all comments due to the high volume we receive. However, we will carefully consider each suggestion."

a Control number		OMB No. 1545-0008	Safe, accurate, FAST! Use IRS e-file	Visit the IRS website at www.irs.gov/efile.
b Employer identification number (EIN)			1 Wages, tips, other compensation	2 Federal income tax withheld
c Employer's name, address, and ZIP code			3 Social security wages	4 Social security tax withheld
			5 Medicare wages and tips	6 Medicare tax withheld
			7 Social security tips	8 Allocated tips
d Employee's social security number			9 Advance EIC payment	10 Dependent care benefits
e Employee's first name and initial Last name Suff.			11 Nonqualified plans	12a See instructions for box 12
			13 Statutory employee / Retirement plan / Third-party sick pay	12b
			14 Other	12c
				12d
f Employee's address and ZIP code				
15 State Employer's state ID number	16 State wages, tips, etc.	17 State income tax	18 Local wages, tips, etc.	19 Local income tax	20 Locality name

Form **W-2** Wage and Tax Statement **2006** Department of the Treasury—Internal Revenue Service

Copy B—To Be Filed With Employee's FEDERAL Tax Return.
This information is being furnished to the Internal Revenue Service.

Form 1040 — U.S. Individual Income Tax Return — 2006

Department of the Treasury—Internal Revenue Service (99) IRS Use Only—Do not write or staple in this space.

For the year Jan. 1–Dec. 31, 2006, or other tax year beginning , 2006, ending , 20

OMB No. 1545-0074

Draft as of 06/21/2006

Label (See instructions on page 16.) Use the IRS label. Otherwise, please print or type.

- Your first name and initial | Last name | Your social security number
- If a joint return, spouse's first name and initial | Last name | Spouse's social security number
- Home address (number and street). If you have a P.O. box, see page 16. | Apt. no.
- City, town or post office, state, and ZIP code. If you have a foreign address, see page 16.

▲ You **must** enter your SSN(s) above. ▲

Checking a box below will not change your tax or refund.

Presidential Election Campaign ▶ Check here if you, or your spouse if filing jointly, want $3 to go to this fund (see page 16) ▶ ☐ You ☐ Spouse

Filing Status
Check only one box.

1. ☐ Single
2. ☐ Married filing jointly (even if only one had income)
3. ☐ Married filing separately. Enter spouse's SSN above and full name here. ▶
4. ☐ Head of household (with qualifying person). (See page 17.) If the qualifying person is a child but not your dependent, enter this child's name here. ▶
5. ☐ Qualifying widow(er) with dependent child (see page 17)

Exemptions

- 6a ☐ **Yourself.** If someone can claim you as a dependent, **do not** check box 6a
- b ☐ **Spouse**
- c **Dependents:**

(1) First name Last name	(2) Dependent's social security number	(3) Dependent's relationship to you	(4) ✓ if qualifying child for child tax credit (see page 19)
			☐
			☐
			☐
			☐

If more than four dependents, see page 19.

Boxes checked on 6a and 6b ____
No. of children on 6c who:
- lived with you ____
- did not live with you due to divorce or separation (see page 20) ____
Dependents on 6c not entered above ____
Add numbers on lines above ▶ ☐

d Total number of exemptions claimed

Income

Attach Form(s) W-2 here. Also attach Forms W-2G and 1099-R if tax was withheld.

If you did not get a W-2, see page 22.

Enclose, but do not attach, any payment. Also, please use Form 1040-V.

- 7 Wages, salaries, tips, etc. Attach Form(s) W-2 . . . . | 7
- 8a **Taxable** interest. Attach Schedule B if required . . . . | 8a
- b **Tax-exempt** interest. **Do not** include on line 8a | 8b
- 9a Ordinary dividends. Attach Schedule B if required . . . . | 9a
- b Qualified dividends (see page 23) | 9b
- 10 Taxable refunds, credits, or offsets of state and local income taxes (see page 23) | 10
- 11 Alimony received . . . . | 11
- 12 Business income or (loss). Attach Schedule C or C-EZ . . . . . . | 12
- 13 Capital gain or (loss). Attach Schedule D if required. If not required, check here ▶ ☐ | 13
- 14 Other gains or (losses). Attach Form 4797 . . . . | 14
- 15a IRA distributions | 15a | b Taxable amount (see page 25) | 15b
- 16a Pensions and annuities | 16a | b Taxable amount (see page 25) | 16b
- 17 Rental real estate, royalties, partnerships, S corporations, trusts, etc. Attach Schedule E | 17
- 18 Farm income or (loss). Attach Schedule F . . . . | 18
- 19 Unemployment compensation . . . . | 19
- 20a Social security benefits | 20a | b Taxable amount (see page 27) | 20b
- 21 Other income. List type and amount (see page 29) _____ | 21
- 22 Add the amounts in the far right column for lines 7 through 21. This is your **total income** ▶ | 22

Adjusted Gross Income

- 23 Archer MSA deduction. Attach Form 8853 . . . . . | 23
- 24 Certain business expenses of reservists, performing artists, and fee-basis government officials. Attach Form 2106 or 2106-EZ | 24
- 25 Health savings account deduction. Attach Form 8889 . . | 25
- 26 Moving expenses. Attach Form 3903 . . . . . . | 26
- 27 One-half of self-employment tax. Attach Schedule SE . . | 27
- 28 Self-employed SEP, SIMPLE, and qualified plans . . . | 28
- 29 Self-employed health insurance deduction (see page 30) . | 29
- 30 Penalty on early withdrawal of savings . . . . . . | 30
- 31a Alimony paid b Recipient's SSN ▶ | 31a
- 32 IRA deduction (see page 31) . . . . | 32
- 33 Student loan interest deduction (see page 33) . . . | 33
- 34 Jury duty pay you gave to your employer . . . . . | 34
- 35 Domestic production activities deduction. Attach Form 8903 | 35
- 36 Add lines 23 through 31a and 32 through 35 . . . . | 36
- 37 Subtract line 36 from line 22. This is your **adjusted gross income** . . . . ▶ | 37

For Disclosure, Privacy Act, and Paperwork Reduction Act Notice, see page 78. Cat. No. 11320B Form **1040** (2006)

Form 1040 (2006) Page **2**

Tax and Credits	38	Amount from line 37 (adjusted gross income)	38	
	39a	Check if: ☐ **You** were born before January 2, 1942, ☐ Blind. } Total boxes checked ▶ 39a		
		☐ **Spouse** was born before January 2, 1942, ☐ Blind. }		
Standard Deduction for—	b	If your spouse itemizes on a separate return or you were a dual-status alien, see page 35 and check here ▶ 39b ☐		
	40	**Itemized deductions** (from Schedule A) **or** your **standard deduction** (see left margin) . .	40	
• People who checked any box on line 39a or 39b **or** who can be claimed as a dependent, see page 36.	41	Subtract line 40 from line 38	41	
	42	If line 38 is over $112,875, or you provided housing to a person displaced by Hurricane Katrina, see page 37. Otherwise, multiply $3,300 by the total number of exemptions claimed on line 6d	42	
	43	**Taxable income.** Subtract line 42 from line 41. If line 42 is more than line 41, enter -0- .	43	
	44	**Tax** (see page 37). Check if any tax is from: **a** ☐ Form(s) 8814 **b** ☐ Form 4972 . .	44	
	45	**Alternative minimum tax** (see page 39). Attach Form 6251	45	
• All others:	46	Add lines 44 and 45 . . . . ▶	46	
Single or Married filing separately, $5,150	47	Foreign tax credit. Attach Form 1116 if required	47		
	48	Credit for child and dependent care expenses. Attach Form 2441	48		
	49	Credit for the elderly or the disabled. Attach Schedule R .	49		
Married filing jointly or Qualifying widow(er), $10,300	50	Education credits. Attach Form 8863	50		
	51	Retirement savings contributions credit. Attach Form 8880 .	51		
	52	Residential energy credits. Attach Form 5695	52		
	53	Child tax credit (see page XX). Attach Form 8901 if required	53		
Head of household, $7,550	54	Credits from: **a** ☐ Form 8396 **b** ☐ Form 8839 **c** ☐ Form 8859	54		
	55	Other credits: **a** ☐ Form 3800 **b** ☐ Form 8801 **c** ☐ Form	55		
	56	Add lines 47 through 55. These are your **total credits**	56	
	57	Subtract line 56 from line 46. If line 56 is more than line 46, enter -0- . . . . ▶	57	
Other Taxes	58	Self-employment tax. Attach Schedule SE	58	
	59	Social security and Medicare tax on tip income not reported to employer. Attach Form 4137 . .	59	
	60	Additional tax on IRAs, other qualified retirement plans, etc. Attach Form 5329 if required . .	60	
	61	Advance earned income credit payments from Form(s) W-2, box 9	61	
	62	Household employment taxes. Attach Schedule H	62	
	63	Add lines 57 through 62. This is your **total tax** . . . . ▶	63	
Payments	64	Federal income tax withheld from Forms W-2 and 1099 . .	64		
	65	2006 estimated tax payments and amount applied from 2005 return	65		
If you have a qualifying child, attach Schedule EIC.	66a	**Earned income credit (EIC)**	66a		
	b	Nontaxable combat pay election ▶	66b			
	67	Excess social security and tier 1 RRTA tax withheld (see page 59)	67		
	68	Additional child tax credit. Attach Form 8812	68		
	69	Amount paid with request for extension to file (see page 59)	69		
	70	Payments from: **a** ☐ Form 2439 **b** ☐ Form 4136 **c** ☐ Form 8885	70		
	71	Credit for federal telephone excise tax paid. Attach Form 8913 if required	71		
	72	Add lines 64, 65, 66a, and 67 through 71. These are your **total payments** . . . . ▶	72	
Refund Direct deposit? See page 59 and fill in 74b, 74c, and 74d, or Form 8888.	73	If line 72 is more than line 63, subtract line 63 from line 72. This is the amount you **overpaid**	73	
	74a	Amount of line 73 you want **refunded to you.** If Form 8888 is attached, check here ▶ ☐	74a	
	▶ b	Routing number	▶ c Type: ☐ Checking ☐ Savings		
	▶ d	Account number			
	75	Amount of line 73 you want **applied to your 2007 estimated tax** ▶	75		
Amount You Owe	76	**Amount you owe.** Subtract line 72 from line 63. For details on how to pay, see page 60 ▶	76	
	77	Estimated tax penalty (see page 60)	77		
Third Party Designee	Do you want to allow another person to discuss this return with the IRS (see page 61)? ☐ **Yes.** Complete the following. ☐ **No**			
	Designee's name ▶	Phone no. ▶ ( )	Personal identification number (PIN) ▶		

Sign Here
Joint return? See page 17.
Keep a copy for your records.

Under penalties of perjury, I declare that I have examined this return and accompanying schedules and statements, and to the best of my knowledge and belief, they are true, correct, and complete. Declaration of preparer (other than taxpayer) is based on all information of which preparer has any knowledge.

Your signature	Date	Your occupation	Daytime phone number ( )
Spouse's signature. If a joint return, **both** must sign.	Date	Spouse's occupation	

Paid Preparer's Use Only

Preparer's signature ▶	Date	Check if self-employed ☐	Preparer's SSN or PTIN
Firm's name (or yours if self-employed), address, and ZIP code ▶		EIN	
		Phone no. ( )	

Form **1040** (2006)

Printed on recycled paper

56 Clergy Tax 2007

Schedule A—Itemized Deductions

SCHEDULES A&B (Form 1040)
Department of the Treasury
Internal Revenue Service (99)

(Schedule B is on back)
▶ Attach to Form 1040.   ▶ See Instructions for Schedules A&B (Form 1040).

OMB No. 1545-0074
2006
Attachment Sequence No. 07

Name(s) shown on Form 1040

Your social security number

Draft as of 06/08/2006

Medical and Dental Expenses		**Caution.** Do not include expenses reimbursed or paid by others.	
	1	Medical and dental expenses (see page A-2)	1
	2	Enter amount from Form 1040, line 38 [2]	
	3	Multiply line 2 by 7.5% (.075)	3
	4	Subtract line 3 from line 1. If line 3 is more than line 1, enter -0-	4
Taxes You Paid (See page A-2.)	5	State and local income taxes	5
	6	Real estate taxes (see page A-5)	6
	7	Personal property taxes	7
	8	Other taxes. List type and amount ▶	8
	9	Add lines 5 through 8	9
Interest You Paid (See page A-5.) **Note.** Personal interest is not deductible.	10	Home mortgage interest and points reported to you on Form 1098	10
	11	Home mortgage interest not reported to you on Form 1098. If paid to the person from whom you bought the home, see page A-6 and show that person's name, identifying no., and address ▶	11
	12	Points not reported to you on Form 1098. See page A-6 for special rules	12
	13	Investment interest. Attach Form 4952 if required. (See page A-6.)	13
	14	Add lines 10 through 13	14
Gifts to Charity If you made a gift and got a benefit for it, see page A-7.	15	Gifts by cash or check. If you made any gift of $250 or more, see page A-7	15
	16	Other than by cash or check. If any gift of $250 or more, see page A-7. You **must** attach Form 8283 if over $500	16
	17	Carryover from prior year	17
	18	Add lines 15 through 17	18
Casualty and Theft Losses	19	Casualty or theft loss(es). Attach Form 4684. (See page A-8.)	19
Job Expenses and Certain Miscellaneous Deductions (See page A-8.)	20	Unreimbursed employee expenses—job travel, union dues, job education, etc. Attach Form 2106 or 2106-EZ if required. (See page A-8.) ▶	20
	21	Tax preparation fees	21
	22	Other expenses—investment, safe deposit box, etc. List type and amount ▶	22
	23	Add lines 20 through 22	23
	24	Enter amount from Form 1040, line 38 [24]	
	25	Multiply line 24 by 2% (.02)	25
	26	Subtract line 25 from line 23. If line 25 is more than line 23, enter -0-	26
Other Miscellaneous Deductions	27	Other—from list on page A-9. List type and amount ▶	27
Total Itemized Deductions	28	Is Form 1040, line 38, over $150,500 (over $75,250 if married filing separately)? ☐ **No.** Your deduction is not limited. Add the amounts in the far right column for lines 4 through 27. Also, enter this amount on Form 1040, line 40. ▶ ☐ **Yes.** Your deduction may be limited. See page A-9 for the amount to enter.	28
	29	If you elect to itemize deductions even though they are less than your standard deduction, check here ▶ ☐	

For Paperwork Reduction Act Notice, see Form 1040 instructions.   Cat. No. 11330X   Schedule A (Form 1040) 2006

Appendix Three 57

Schedules A&B (Form 1040) 2006 — OMB No. 1545-0074 — Page **2**

Name(s) shown on Form 1040. Do not enter name and social security number if shown on other side. | Your social security number

Schedule B—Interest and Ordinary Dividends

Attachment Sequence No. **08**

Part I
Interest

(See page B-1 and the instructions for Form 1040, line 8a.)

Note. If you received a Form 1099-INT, Form 1099-OID, or substitute statement from a brokerage firm, list the firm's name as the payer and enter the total interest shown on that form.

1 List name of payer. If any interest is from a seller-financed mortgage and the buyer used the property as a personal residence, see page B-1 and list this interest first. Also, show that buyer's social security number and address ▶

	Amount
1	

2 Add the amounts on line 1 . . . . | 2 |
3 Excludable interest on series EE and I U.S. savings bonds issued after 1989. Attach Form 8815 . . . . | 3 |
4 Subtract line 3 from line 2. Enter the result here and on Form 1040, line 8a ▶ | 4 |

Note. If line 4 is over $1,500, you must complete Part III.

Part II
Ordinary Dividends

(See page B-1 and the instructions for Form 1040, line 9a.)

Note. If you received a Form 1099-DIV or substitute statement from a brokerage firm, list the firm's name as the payer and enter the ordinary dividends shown on that form.

5 List name of payer ▶

	Amount
5	

6 Add the amounts on line 5. Enter the total here and on Form 1040, line 9a . ▶ | 6 |

Note. If line 6 is over $1,500, you must complete Part III.

Part III
Foreign Accounts and Trusts

(See page B-2.)

You must complete this part if you **(a)** had over $1,500 of taxable interest or ordinary dividends; or **(b)** had a foreign account; or **(c)** received a distribution from, or were a grantor of, or a transferor to, a foreign trust.

	Yes	No

7a At any time during 2006, did you have an interest in or a signature or other authority over a financial account in a foreign country, such as a bank account, securities account, or other financial account? See page B-2 for exceptions and filing requirements for Form TD F 90-22.1 . . . .

b If "Yes," enter the name of the foreign country ▶

8 During 2006, did you receive a distribution from, or were you the grantor of, or transferor to, a foreign trust? If "Yes," you may have to file Form 3520. See page B-2 . . . .

For Paperwork Reduction Act Notice, see Form 1040 instructions.   Schedule B (Form 1040) 2006

Printed on recycled paper

Draft as of 06/08/2006

SCHEDULE SE
(Form 1040)

Department of the Treasury
Internal Revenue Service (99)

Self-Employment Tax

▶ Attach to Form 1040. ▶ See Instructions for Schedule SE (Form 1040).

OMB No. 1545-0074

2006

Attachment Sequence No. **17**

Name of person with **self-employment** income (as shown on Form 1040) | Social security number of person with **self-employment** income ▶

Who Must File Schedule SE

You must file Schedule SE if:

- You had net earnings from self-employment from **other than** church employee income (line 4 of Short Schedule SE or line 4c of Long Schedule SE) of $400 or more, **or**
- You had church employee income of $108.28 or more. Income from services you performed as a minister or a member of a religious order **is not** church employee income (see page SE-1).

Note. Even if you had a loss or a small amount of income from self-employment, it may be to your benefit to file Schedule SE and use either "optional method" in Part II of Long Schedule SE (see page SE-3).

Exception. If your only self-employment income was from earnings as a minister, member of a religious order, or Christian Science practitioner **and** you filed Form 4361 and received IRS approval not to be taxed on those earnings, **do not** file Schedule SE. Instead, write "Exempt–Form 4361" on Form 1040, line 58.

May I Use Short Schedule SE or Must I Use Long Schedule SE?

Note. Use this flowchart **only if** you must file Schedule SE. If unsure, see Who Must File Schedule SE, above.

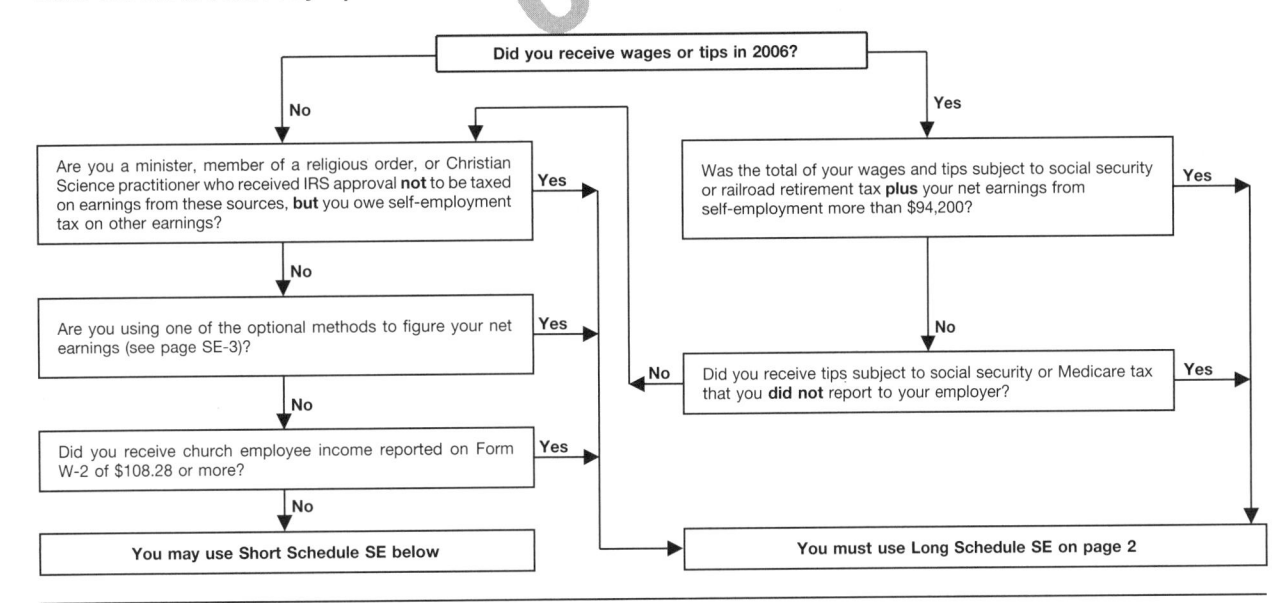

```
                    ┌─────────────────────────────────┐
                    │ Did you receive wages or tips in 2006? │
                    └─────────────────────────────────┘
                         │ No                    │ Yes
                         ▼                        ▼
┌──────────────────────────────────┐    ┌──────────────────────────────────┐
│ Are you a minister, member of a  │    │ Was the total of your wages and  │  Yes
│ religious order, or Christian    │Yes │ tips subject to social security  │─────▶
│ Science practitioner who received│───▶│ or railroad retirement tax plus  │
│ IRS approval not to be taxed on  │    │ your net earnings from           │
│ earnings from these sources, but │    │ self-employment more than $94,200?│
│ you owe self-employment tax on   │    └──────────────────────────────────┘
│ other earnings?                  │              │ No
└──────────────────────────────────┘              ▼
         │ No                          ┌──────────────────────────────────┐
         ▼                             │ Did you receive tips subject to  │ Yes
┌──────────────────────────────────┐   │ social security or Medicare tax  │─────▶
│ Are you using one of the optional│Yes│ that you did not report to your  │
│ methods to figure your net       │──▶│ employer?                        │
│ earnings (see page SE-3)?        │No │                                  │
└──────────────────────────────────┘◀──└──────────────────────────────────┘
         │ No
         ▼
┌──────────────────────────────────┐
│ Did you receive church employee  │ Yes
│ income reported on Form W-2 of   │─────▶
│ $108.28 or more?                 │
└──────────────────────────────────┘
         │ No
         ▼
┌──────────────────────────────────┐    ┌──────────────────────────────────┐
│ You may use Short Schedule SE below│    │ You must use Long Schedule SE on page 2 │
└──────────────────────────────────┘    └──────────────────────────────────┘
```

Section A—Short Schedule SE. Caution. Read above to see if you can use Short Schedule SE.

1	Net farm profit or (loss) from Schedule F, line 36, and farm partnerships, Schedule K-1 (Form 1065), box 14, code A	1
2	Net profit or (loss) from Schedule C, line 31; Schedule C-EZ, line 3; Schedule K-1 (Form 1065), box 14, code A (other than farming); and Schedule K-1 (Form 1065-B), box 9, code J1. Ministers and members of religious orders, see page SE-1 for amounts to report on this line. See page SE-2 for other income to report	2
3	Combine lines 1 and 2	3
4	**Net earnings from self-employment.** Multiply line 3 by 92.35% (.9235). If less than $400, **do not** file this schedule; you do not owe self-employment tax . . . . ▶	4
5	**Self-employment tax.** If the amount on line 4 is: • $94,200 or less, multiply line 4 by 15.3% (.153). Enter the result here and on **Form 1040, line 58.** • More than $94,200, multiply line 4 by 2.9% (.029). Then, add $11,680.80 to the result. Enter the total here and on **Form 1040, line 58.**	5
6	**Deduction for one-half of self-employment tax.** Multiply line 5 by 50% (.5). Enter the result here and on **Form 1040, line 27**	6	

For Paperwork Reduction Act Notice, see Form 1040 instructions. Cat. No. 11358Z **Schedule SE (Form 1040) 2006**

Schedule SE (Form 1040) 2006 — Attachment Sequence No. 17 — Page 2

Name of person with **self-employment** income (as shown on Form 1040) | Social security number of person with **self-employment** income ▶

Section B—Long Schedule SE

Part I — Self-Employment Tax

Note. If your only income subject to self-employment tax is **church employee income,** skip lines 1 through 4b. Enter -0- on line 4c and go to line 5a. Income from services you performed as a minister or a member of a religious order **is not** church employee income. See page SE-1.

A If you are a minister, member of a religious order, or Christian Science practitioner **and** you filed Form 4361, but you had $400 or more of **other** net earnings from self-employment, check here and continue with Part I . . . . . . ▶ ☐

1. Net farm profit or (loss) from Schedule F, line 36, and farm partnerships, Schedule K-1 (Form 1065), box 14, code A. **Note.** Skip this line if you use the farm optional method (see page SE-4) — **1**

2. Net profit or (loss) from Schedule C, line 31; Schedule C-EZ, line 3; Schedule K-1 (Form 1065), box 14, code A (other than farming); and Schedule K-1 (Form 1065-B), box 9, code J1. Ministers and members of religious orders, see page SE-1 for amounts to report on this line. See page SE-2 for other income to report. **Note.** Skip this line if you use the nonfarm optional method (see page SE-4) — **2**

3. Combine lines 1 and 2 — **3**

4a. If line 3 is more than zero, multiply line 3 by 92.35% (.9235). Otherwise, enter amount from line 3 — **4a**

   b. If you elect one or both of the optional methods, enter the total of lines 15 and 17 here — **4b**

   c. Combine lines 4a and 4b. If less than $400, **stop;** you do not owe self-employment tax. **Exception.** If less than $400 and you had **church employee income,** enter -0- and continue. ▶ **4c**

5a. Enter your **church employee income** from Form W-2. See page SE-1 for definition of church employee income — **5a**

   b. Multiply line 5a by 92.35% (.9235). If less than $100, enter -0- — **5b**

6. **Net earnings from self-employment.** Add lines 4c and 5b — **6**

7. Maximum amount of combined wages and self-employment earnings subject to social security tax or the 6.2% portion of the 7.65% railroad retirement (tier 1) tax for 2006 — **7** | 94,200 | 00

8a. Total social security wages and tips (total of boxes 3 and 7 on Form(s) W-2) and railroad retirement (tier 1) compensation. If $94,200 or more, skip lines 8b through 10, and go to line 11 — **8a**

   b. Unreported tips subject to social security tax (from Form 4137, line 9) — **8b**

   c. Add lines 8a and 8b — **8c**

9. Subtract line 8c from line 7. If zero or less, enter -0- here and on line 10 and go to line 11 ▶ **9**

10. Multiply the **smaller** of line 6 or line 9 by 12.4% (.124) — **10**

11. Multiply line 6 by 2.9% (.029) — **11**

12. **Self-employment tax.** Add lines 10 and 11. Enter here and on **Form 1040, line 58** — **12**

13. **Deduction for one-half of self-employment tax.** Multiply line 12 by 50% (.5). Enter the result here and on **Form 1040, line 27** — **13**

Part II — Optional Methods To Figure Net Earnings (see page SE-3)

Farm Optional Method. You may use this method **only** if **(a)** your gross farm income[1] was not more than $2,400, **or (b)** your net farm profits[2] were less than $1,733.

14. Maximum income for optional methods — **14** | 1,600 | 00

15. Enter the **smaller** of: two-thirds (⅔) of gross farm income[1] (not less than zero) **or** $1,600. Also include this amount on line 4b above — **15**

Nonfarm Optional Method. You may use this method **only** if **(a)** your net nonfarm profits[3] were less than $1,733 and also less than 72.189% of your gross nonfarm income,[4] **and (b)** you had net earnings from self-employment of at least $400 in 2 of the prior 3 years.

Caution. You may use this method no more than five times.

16. Subtract line 15 from line 14 — **16**

17. Enter the **smaller** of: two-thirds (⅔) of gross nonfarm income[4] (not less than zero) **or** the amount on line 16. Also include this amount on line 4b above — **17**

[1] From Sch. F, line 11, and Sch. K-1 (Form 1065), box 14, code B.
[2] From Sch. F, line 36, and Sch. K-1 (Form 1065), box 14, code A.
[3] From Sch. C, line 31; Sch. C-EZ, line 3; Sch. K-1 (Form 1065), box 14, code A; and Sch. K-1 (Form 1065-B), box 9, code J1.
[4] From Sch. C, line 7; Sch. C-EZ, line 1; Sch. K-1 (Form 1065), box 14, code C; and Sch. K-1 (Form 1065-B), box 9, code J2.

Schedule SE (Form 1040) 2006

Printed on recycled paper

APPENDIX FOUR

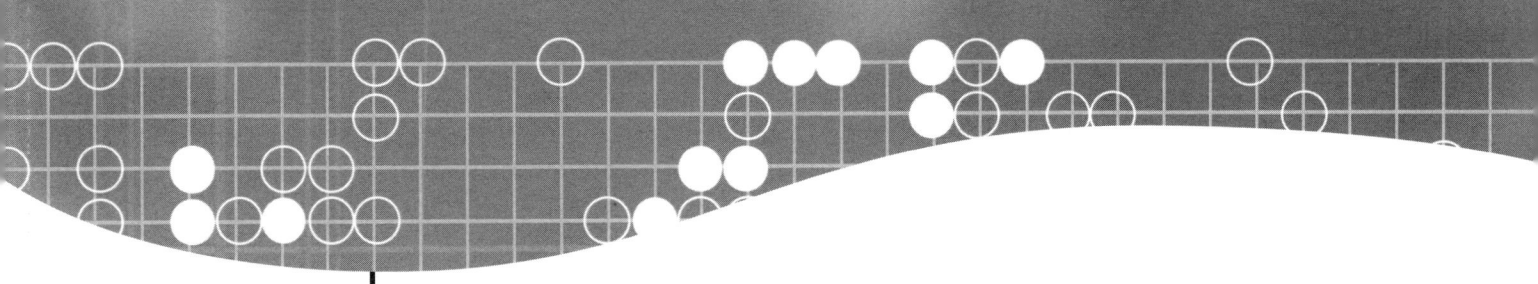

HOW TO HANDLE 1099s

Important: This section only applies if you received a 1099 and *not* a W-2 from your church.

If you are a minister who received a 1099 instead of a W-2, begin by filling out the income worksheet for Box 1 on page 10; then enter that number where indicated below:

$_____ **Total from W-2 Income Worksheet**

$_____ **Health-Insurance Premiums Paid for You by the Church**

$_____ **Health-Expense Reimbursements** (This includes payment of insurance deductibles, co-insurance amounts and any other out-of-pocket expenses paid for you by the church.)

=$_____ **Total** (This is the number that should appear on Line 7 of your Form-1099 MISC given to you by the church.)

✏️ Enter this number on Schedule C, Line 1.

If you received offerings and honorariums paid to you as a guest speaker (these are monies where your offering check was made out to *you* [e.g., "John Smith"] and not your ministry [e.g., "John Smith Ministries"] and not to your church, write that amount here:

$_____

✏️ Add this number to any amount on Schedule C, Line 1.

Note: Sometimes a church where you speak will ask you to fill out a Form W-9 so that they have your Social Security number for the 1099.

WHAT DOESN'T GO ON FORM 1099-MISC, LINE 7

If you get a 1099, here's what *doesn't* go on Form 1099-MISC, Line 7:

- **Offerings and Honorariums to You as a Guest Speaker, in Which the Check Is Made Out to Your Ministry** (e.g., "John Smith Ministries, Inc.") **or to Your Church.**
- **Offerings and Honorariums to You as a Guest Speaker, in Which the Check is Made Out to You Personally** (e.g.,

"John Smith") *but* the Amount is designated as Housing allowance (e.g., "housing allowance for Pastor John Smith"—this can be done on the check itself), as long as you actually spent the money on housing items.

If you received a 1099 for either of the above two situations, it needs to be corrected by the church that gave it to you. If that is not possible, you can try using the "nominee 1099" procedure. To do this, follow the five steps as outlined here and attach a schedule to your tax return with the information as noted.

Step 1
Enter a total of the amounts shown on all Forms 1099 you received.
Step 2
Add to this any amounts which you must report from other sources for which you did not receive 1099 Forms.
Step 3
Show the amounts from the 1099s that you should not have received, and subtract it from the total.
Step 4
Identify this adjustment as a "Nominee Distribution" or other appropriate designation.
Step 5
Report the adjusted total on Schedule C, Line 1 *or* on Form 1040, Line 21, whichever applies to you.

You may want to add a note to the schedule explaining why the 1099 should not have been issued to you.

Important: You won't find the "nominee 1099" procedure in any IRS publication (I've looked). They do have a similar procedure for Schedule B, from which the above is adapted. I have seen some ministers' returns prepared using the IRS procedure and reporting the 1099s less the extra income on Schedule B, and this appeared to have worked. The "nominee 1099" procedure has the advantage of being a schedule to your return clearly showing what happened, along with an explanatory note. On the other hand, a CPA who used the Schedule B procedure told me he thought because the IRS was used to seeing nominee distributions on Schedule B, it was less likely to be flagged. This situation happens so rarely it's hard to say which would be better in a given situation, so you should pick whichever one you're more comfortable with.

Tip: Only those who get a W-2 escape taxation on church-provided health plans. (I don't care what your accountant told you!)

1099s AND FRINGE BENEFITS

There are three major exceptions to the rule that ministers on 1099s don't get fringe benefits:

1. The 403(b) church retirement plan (due to a recent tax law change)
2. The child-care benefit
3. Employer-provided educational assistance

Even on these, not everyone agrees that these benefits are tax free for a minister who receives a 1099. Although the IRS took the position in the past that church retirement plans are not available to ministers on 1099s on a tax-free basis, a new law changed that position. The general rule is that it is better to get a W-2 in order to enjoy tax-free fringe benefits.

HELPFUL HINTS

- If you received a 1099, other than the differences just explained, simply go through Part 1 of this book to finish your return—but note that if you get a 1099, Box 7 (ministers professional expenses) are entered on Schedule C, and Box 11 (business auto expenses) are entered on Schedule C, Line 9.
- You do not need to attach a 1099 to your tax return unless Line 4 of the 1099 shows Federal Income Tax withheld. If this is the case, carry the number from Form 1099, Line 4 to Form 1040, Line 64 and then attach a copy of the 1099 to your return.

Important Information About the Deason Rule (aka the Dalan Rule)

If you have received a 1099 and have business expenses that have not been reimbursed by the church—*and* you also receive a housing allowance, the Deason, or Dalan, Rule applies to you. Put simply:

> The IRS will reduce the amount of business expenses you can deduct by the percentage of your income that is housing allowance.

I personally don't agree with this rule for technical reasons, because housing allowance paid to a minister, must, by definition, be spent only on housing-related items to be excludible. Thus, it follows that all expenditures for ordinary and necessary business expenses have to have been made out of ordinary income, and should therefore be deductible. Business expenses of a minister cannot, by the very nature of the housing allowance itself, be attributable to earning income which is exempt from tax. However, it is my duty to inform you that if you as a minister:

- Receive a 1099 (or no reporting form of any kind at all),
- Receive a housing allowance, and
- Have church-related business expenses that you paid for out of your own pocket and for which the church has not reimbursed you,

the IRS is going to take the position that this rule applies to you. Here's how it works:

Let's say your housing allowance is $10,000 (this could be what was paid to you, or it can also be the value of a parsonage that the church owned and you lived in). Let's say your salary is $40,000.

The IRS will divide your $10,000 housing allowance by your $50,000 compensation (salary plus housing), and come up with a 20% percentage. This means they will disallow 20 percent of your business expense deductions under this rule.

Now let's say you have $5,000 of business expenses that you were going to deduct on your Schedule C. Current law says you have to reduce that $5,000 by 20%. That comes out to $1,000, and leaves you with only $4,000 of expenses that you can actually deduct.

For many ministers, that means you will pay $300 more in taxes than you would have if you had gotten a W-2 and the church had simply reimbursed you for your business expenses.

Tip: Want a perfectly legal tax loophole to get out of the Deason Rule? Have your church start reporting your salary on a W-2 and then have your church set up an accountable reimbursement policy. This way, when the church reimburses you for church-related expenses, they don't show up on your W-2, and the Deason Rule doesn't apply to you at all. All perfectly legal, tax smart—and fully IRS approved.

KEEP YOUR CHURCH ON THE CUTTING EDGE

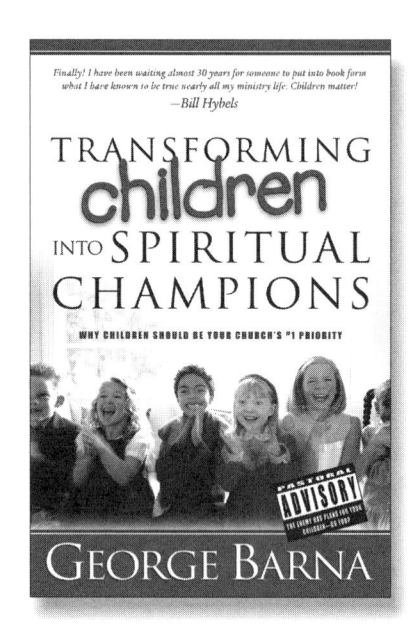

Transforming Children into Spiritual Champions
Why Children Should Be Your Church's #1 Priority
George Barna
ISBN 08307.32934

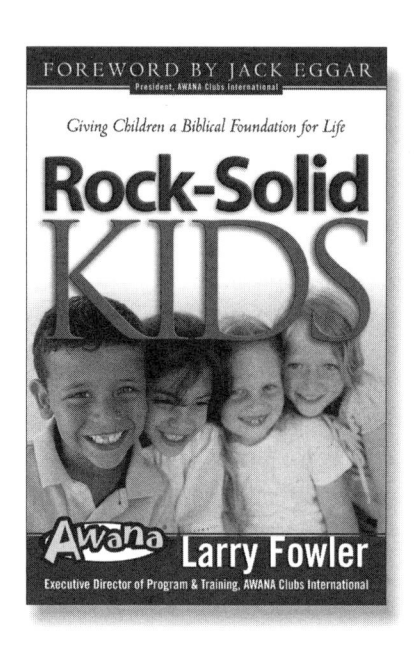

Rock-Solid Kids
Giving Children a Biblical Foundation for Life
Larry Fowler
ISBN 08307.37138

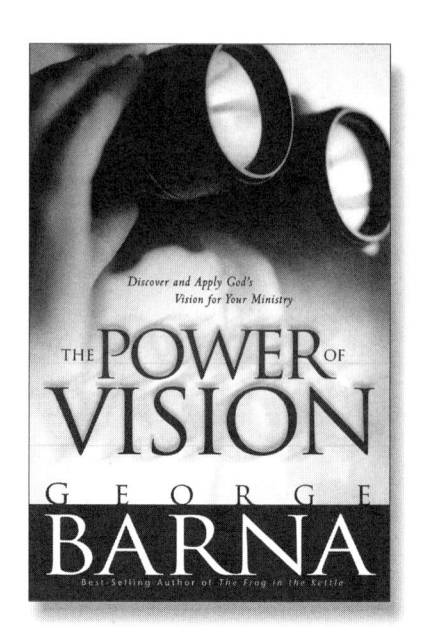

The Power of Vision
Discover and Apply God's Vision for Your Ministry
George Barna
ISBN 08307.32551

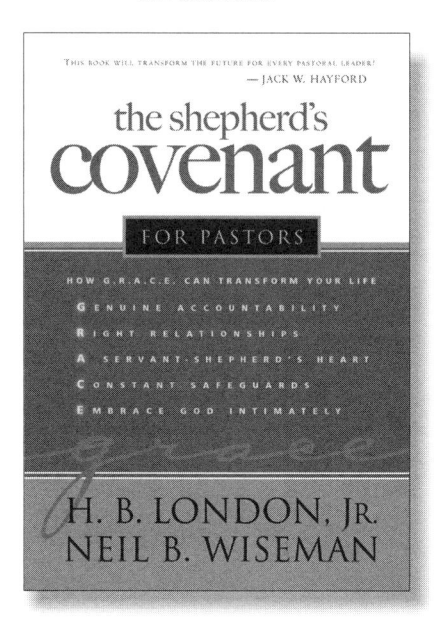

The Shepherd's Covenant for Pastors
How G.R.A.C.E. Can Transform Your Life
H.B. London, Jr. and Neil B. Wiseman
ISBN 08307.37405

The Habits of Highly Effective Churches
Being Strategic in Your God-Given Ministry
George Barna
ISBN 08307.18605

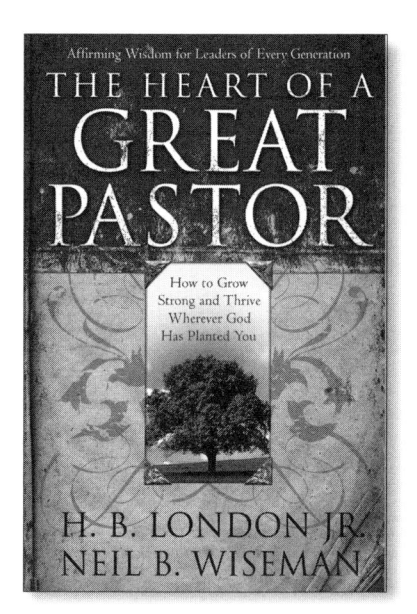

The Heart of a Great Pastor
How to Grow Strong and Thrive Wherever God Has Planted You
H.B. London Jr. and Neil B. Wiseman
ISBN 08307.42816

Available at bookstores everywhere!

Visit **www.regalbooks.com** to join **Regal's FREE e-newsletter**. You'll get useful **excerpts from our newest releases** and **special access to online chats with your favorite authors**. Sign up today!

Regal
God's Word for Your World™
www.regalbooks.com